GEORGE
LUCAS

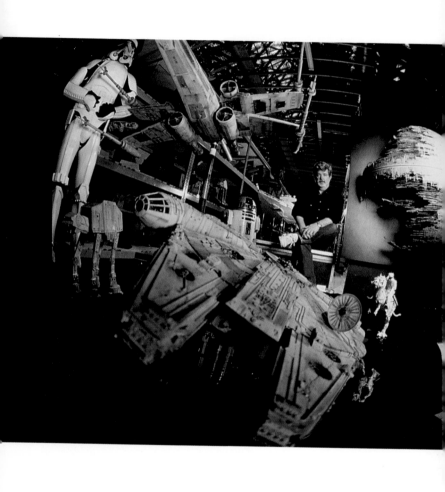

GEORGE LUCAS

Chris Salewicz

ORION

First published in 1998 by Orion Media

An imprint of Orion Books Ltd

Orion House, 5 Upper St Martin's Lane, London WC2H 9EA

Project editor: Natasha Martyn-Johns

Designed by Leigh Jones

A CIP catalogue record for this book is available
from the British Library.

ISBN 0 75281 318 8

Printed and bound in Italy

CONTENTS

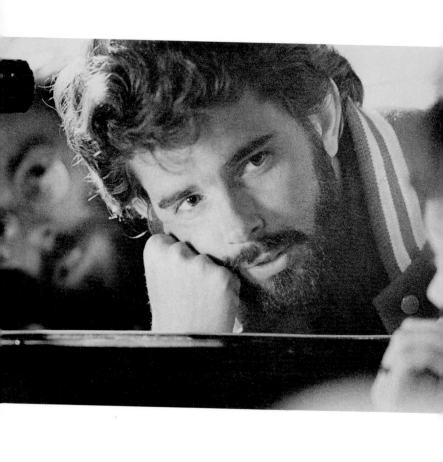

1 The Cruiser and the Force

In the late afternoon of Tuesday 12 June 1962, George Lucas drove towards his parents' home from the Modesto city library. The eighteen-year-old Californian was in his Fiat Bianchina, the tiny Italian car whose two-stroke engine he had stripped down and souped up until it was a fizzing, feisty lump of powerful metal. He had added an anti-roll bar and cut a sunroof into the top of the vehicle.

Like his biker friends at Modesto's Round Table hamburger joint, George Lucas affected greased-back hair and blue jeans, living the kind of Californian cruising lifestyle celebrated in the hotrodding songs just beginning to be recorded by the Beach Boys and Jan and Dean. That afternoon, however, he almost hit his own Dead Man's Curve. Swinging off the blacktop onto the dirt road that led to the Lucas family house, the setting sun obscuring his vision, he was sideswiped by a Chevrolet Impala. Flipping over, the tiny Fiat rolled like a tumbleweed towards a grove of walnut trees. The force of the impact tore apart his seat-belt — he was catapulted through the open sunroof and knocked unconscious as the car came to a halt by crumpling around a tree-trunk.

By the time an ambulance arrived, it seemed George Lucas was dead: he was not breathing and there was no sign of a heartbeat. When he eventually reached hospital, it was found that he had undergone huge internal bleeding. The four months he spent in bed recovering utterly altered his life. 'Before that,' said Lucas, 'I just went with what I enjoyed. I sat down that summer and did a lot of meditating on what I was here for.'

Would it be too fanciful to see a mortally injured Luke Skywalker lying in that hospital bed in the small northern Californian town of Modesto, grappling with notions of an energy field that binds the galaxy together? The idea that the Force may be with us is, after all, the most profound legacy of the *Star Wars* trilogy of films, the first of which George Lucas would unveil in 1977, that year of pivotal change that also brought us the earthquake of punk rock.

The George Lucas paradox could hardly be more marked: on one hand the *Star Wars* films sold over $3 billion worth of merchandising; on the other they offered in the Force, loosely interpreted as the power everyone has and seldom uses, a life philosophy that was sufficiently ambiguous and catch-all to make some considerable difference to the quality of thinking and existence in the last quarter of the twentieth century – and, we suspect, beyond that time as well. Darth Vader, meanwhile, entered the popular imagination as a synonym for all that was dark and diabolic. (So much so, indeed, that when James Earl Jones, the actor who played his voice, provided voice-overs on a series of American AT&T television advertisements, it was as though an extraordinary cultural confusion had been triggered off.)

At a lesser level, George Lucas, the architect of a profound way of thinking that is also populist as it could be, is the man who utterly altered cinema, the director-producer who introduced blockbuster event movies.

Yet this was from a director who believed his first talent to be editing. Lucas found himself to have an extraordinary sensibility for film that was literally at a frame-by-frame level, a gift with which Walt Disney also had been blessed, but, he feared, a weakness in character and narrative. To cover this perceived personal artistic flaw, he developed the use of unique soundtracks, skilled graphics and, above all, unprecedentedly fast cutting, becoming an innovator of a style taken up wholesale by video makers.

Deeply committed to what the musician Prince defined as positivity, Lucas equally has an almost Howard Hughes-like image, reminiscent of a grouchy Old Testament prophet, or, perhaps, Profit – if you're not careful, the P word can loom large in Lucas discussions: Largest Grossing This . . . Top Film of That . . . Billions Earned . . . Yet so much of this colossal amount of cash has been put into Skywalker ranch, to create even more billions – for this is the home of George Lucas and Lucasfilm, with its very lucrative Industrial Light and Magic (ILM) offshoot, another well of creativity.

Star Wars turned upside down Hollywood's attitudes towards science fiction; it was partly responsible for the notion of the Feelgood film; it changed the industry's definition of the spring and summer market; it re-established symphonic music in films and gave new importance to sound; it exploded the boundaries of special effects; it made merchandising the characters from a movie as important as the movie itself; it created a pop mythology, and

– as we have said – lodged the notion of the Force in the collective psyche.

And all that George Lucas had hoped when making it was that the first film would provide enough money to make a sequel.

2 Film School and THX 1138

George Walton Lucas Jr. was born on 14 May 1944, which was Mother's Day that year in the United States. He was the third of four children for Dorothy and George Lucas Sr., their only son and the apple of everyone's eye.

Modesto is in northern California, in the flat walnut-growing and wine-making region an hour's drive south of the state capital of Sacramento. The only times the Lucas family would leave the area would be for the annual family pilgrimages to Disneyland. George Lucas Sr. was the son of a Californian oilfield worker; a figure in the community, he had made good by running the local stationery store, which he had been rather hoping that his son would take over from him.

The young George Lucas, who would build soapbox derby racers and other feats of schoolboy engineering in the small shed at the back of the family house, was a thin, somewhat sickly child. This was perhaps because of a predisposition to frailty in the family blood (later George would discover that he was diabetic): his mother was often confined to bed, leaving her husband to care for the children. George, as the only son, experienced an awkward relationship with his well-meaning but martinet-like father (he would be made, for example, to have his head shaved every summer); this became the basis for the good/bad father figures of Obi-Wan Kenobi and Darth Vader.

The school grades of George Lucas Jr. were not impressive. For the most part, in fact, he was a D-student. It was in an effort to prepare himself for his final examinations, in three days' time, that on the day of his near-fatal car crash he had been attempting to study in the Modesto city library.

Like his near-contemporaries John Lennon and Keith Richards on the other side of the Atlantic, George Lucas was one of those children who was unsuited for academic life but could flourish in an artistic environment. Unlike those two examples, his desire to attend art school was not consummated: his strict father refused to cough up the money for any such course. George's interest in photography offered another route, however. Inspired by a friendship he had struck up with the celebrated cinematographer Haskell Wexler (whom he had met while attempting a photographic essay at the auto-shop where Wexler was having a sports car rebuilt), he had decided to go to film school at the University of Southern California in Los Angeles, thinking this was the closest he could come to a photography course.

In 1964 he signed up for classes in the history of film and animation, as well as the subsidiary subjects of English and astronomy. Unlike most of his young film-directing peers, Lucas up to that point had had little interest in pictures: his periodic excursions to Modesto's movie theatres largely had been a pretext for trying to pick up girls. But at USC he found himself: at the end of the first year, betraying the impetus that had made him sign up for the course by using a set of still photographs, he made a minute-long film that won awards at eighteen film festivals. 'Everything I did was involved with film and I couldn't think of anything else,' he said. *Freiheit*, which he made in the Malibu hills, was another short, about a man escaping from East to West Germany. This theme of a man breaking free of his past, which was to dominate the work of the student who had fled small-town Modesto, reappeared in *THX 1138: 4HB*, which he made in 1967 as a graduate student. Cannily linking up with navy cinema students, because they had access to colour film, Lucas constructed a short picture that used a wild mixture of Bach and indistinguishable air traffic control voices as the audio bed for the story of a man escaping a mechanized society. Shot in underground parking lots and other symbols of dehumanized society, the film had a sense of documentary about it: the framing was deliberately never perfect – in a sense that would prevail in Lucas's larger work. At the National Student Film Festival *THX 1138: 4HB* won the award for Best Drama.

In turn, it helped Lucas win a further award, from Columbia, to shoot a short film about the making of the western *McKenna's Gold*, which was being produced by Carl Foreman. More importantly, he also picked up the Samuel Warner scholarship offered by Warner Brothers: one student a year was allowed to work at the studio for six months. (Before he took this up, Lucas felt he should no longer delay the inevitable, and presented himself at his local draft board, expecting all along that he might be sent to Vietnam. It was then that to his amazement he found he was classified 4F at his medical – because he was diabetic.)

With suitable symbolism, George Lucas arrived at Warner Brothers on the day that Jack Warner cleared out his office and left, the venerable studio having been bought by a television packaging company. 'The whole place was shutting down, so I couldn't be assigned to the story department. They were only making one movie, *Finian's Rainbow*, so that's where I ended up.'

Finian's Rainbow, a musical about labour exploitation and race relations that had originally debuted on Broadway in 1947, was being directed by Francis Ford Coppola, already something of a legend amongst film school students.

Francis was the first film student to make it into the film business on a direct line, out of film school and into the industry. Other people had graduated, worked as writers for a couple of years and eventually broken in – some people did it through Roger Corman, but that didn't really count. They'd do exploitation films, and nobody ever knew what happened to them. They'd surface maybe ten years later on television, but that wasn't really 'making it'. You see, we were taught, it was the credo of the film school that we had drilled into us every day, that nobody would ever get a job in the industry. You'd graduate from film school and become a ticket-taker at Disneyland, or get a job with some industrial outfit in Kansas. But nobody had ever gotten a job in Hollywood making theatrical films. Then Francis did it, clearly and indisputably, and this happened just when we were in school. He was about five years ahead of me, and he was working on his second film already, his first big feature.

Coppola had not wanted to make *Finian's Rainbow*, but needed the work. The fact that the director and Lucas were about the only people under fifty on the set was not without significance. Without their being aware of it, both men were participants in a pivotal moment of Hollywood history. Not since the period immediately after the Second World War had Hollywood encouraged any new intake of talent into the movie-making business. 'A bit of history opened up like a seam,' said Lucas, 'and as many of us who could crammed in.' Virtually oblivious to the youth explosion triggered off by the 'Swinging' Sixties, the film industry was mired in a moribund conservatism that was deeply suspicious of any youthful newcomers. 'Grow a beard!' suggested the already hirsute Coppola to Lucas. 'It will make people respect you.' By so urging, he helped inspire a somewhat questionable facial fashion among young film-makers that was to linger for at least the next two decades.

At the time, however, Lucas had his own ambitions: 'What I wanted to do was get into the animation department: steal some footage or whatever and start making a film. About three weeks into the picture I told Francis I was bored, but he said, "Look, kid, stick with me, and I'll give you things to do." He did, and it turned out that we complemented each other very well. I was essentially an editor and a cameraman, while Francis is a writer and director – more into actors and acting.'

Coppola has gone on record as saying that Lucas was 'the only person I could talk to'. But wasn't there a more complex chemistry at work here? In *Take One* Lucas told Audie Bock what he perceived to be the essence of their relationship: 'I'm really conservative – he used to call me the seventy-year-old man – and Francis is always sixteen. He's always running off and being crazy. I'm Midwestern American and he's essentially New York Italian-American. It was a good

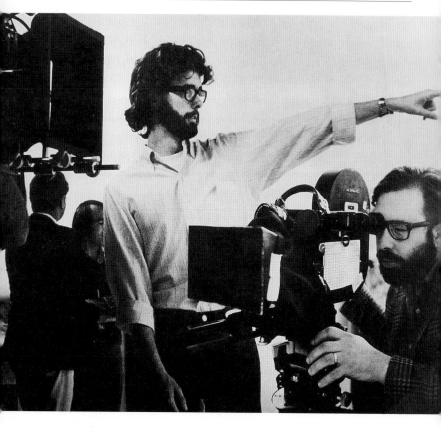

Francis Coppola (right) persuaded Lucas to write the screenplay for THX 1138**. Both are shown here on the set of the film**.

combination, and I started being his assistant.' (It is interesting that for Lucas, Modesto, only eighty miles from San
Francisco, was as far mentally and intellectually from that
free-thinking city as Iowa.)

In July 1968 they made *The Rain People* together. A fascinating road movie, made entirely on location with a
constantly evolving script, the film fell by the wayside in
comparison with *Easy Rider* – perhaps because it suggested
that dropping out was escapism. For Lucas, who was
employed to make a documentary about the making of the
film, the movie held a larger purpose. On the set of *Finian's
Rainbow*, Coppola had kept insisting that if he wanted to
direct he must first learn to write. 'I can't write,' Lucas
complained. 'Yes, you can: I'll help you,' was always
Coppola's response.

Coppola then secured a deal with the new regime at Warner
Brothers to deliver a package of 'youth' movies. There was a
catch here, however: if Warners didn't go for Coppola's product, he would have to repay personally any money advanced.
All the same, it was deemed that Lucas's last student project,
THX 1138: 4HB, should have its title abbreviated to *THX
1138* and be worked up into a full-length feature, to become
the first of these films out of the starting blocks. Accordingly,
with Coppola goading him on, Lucas wrote *THX 1138* each
morning from 4 to 6 a.m. during the production of *The Rain
People*: he had been paid $3,000 as an advance for this script,
which also served as his fee for working on the road movie.
(On a second draft of *THX 1138* he brought in Walter Murch,
an old friend from USC who later edited *Apocalypse Now*.)

Coppola and Lucas had already decided they would go for
the big time, and would set up an independent studio outside

Hollywood. After finishing shooting *The Rain People*, Coppola
visited a film company called Lanterna in Denmark that had
been established in an old mansion. It was this that became
the inspiration for the country-estate headquarters that he
sought for what had now been named American Zoetrope. After
then visiting the Fotokina exhibition in Germany, Coppola
ordered the latest editing equipment from Kem and Steenbeck,
and had it shipped to San Francisco.

But all the bids they made on houses in their favoured
location, the old Marin County town of Ross, fell through.
The new editing equipment was about to arrive, which they
had to use for cutting *The Rain People*, and they had nowhere
even to put it.

Then they found an old warehouse on Folsom Street in the
middle of San Francisco. Moving in 'temporarily', they soon
discovered that the costs of refurbishing the warehouse had
eaten up all the money from the Warners development deal,
and they couldn't move elsewhere. However, Coppola liked
being there in the city's 'bohemian atmosphere'. Later he
bought property in Mill Valley, where Lucas could live and
work in the heat of which he was so fond.

('As soon as we got set up,' said Lucas to Audie Bock. 'I
started pulling in all of my school friends – Bill Huyck and
Gloria Katz, John Milius, Matt Robbins [*Corvette Summer*],
Hal Barwood [producer of *Corvette Summer* and co-scenar-
ist with Robbins on Spielberg's *Sugarland Express*]. We were
all outsiders banding together again, and the group came to
include Marty Scorsese and Brian de Palma, who were in the
same situation in New York.')

THX 1138 was shot in San Francisco's just-completed Bay
Area subway system – the concrete wastelands are turned

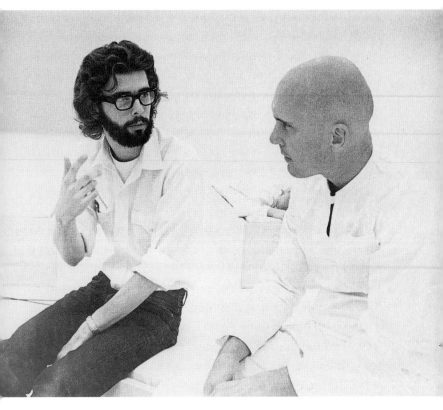

With Robert Duvall on the set of THX 1138.

into an endless white set, against which are juxtaposed the entirely white-clad characters. Lucas improvised the explosions in the plot, on a miniature set that he built himself, with ten dollars' worth of fireworks. The film starred Robert Duvall as an outlaw hounded by robot police after he and Maggie McOmie have fallen in love, sex being banned in this test-tube world. A bleak but believable picture that also starred Donald Pleasence, it is often visually extraordinary as images are played out from different perspectives. Warners loathed it.

Ted Ashley was now in charge of Warners, which had been taken over by the Kinney Parking Corporation. Ashley considered Lucas's cut of *THX 1138* to be disturbingly uncommercial. So, for the first time in Warners' history – though perhaps setting a precedent for what was to become a standard film-making practice – a film was taken away from its director and producer; *THX 1138* was passed over to Rudi Fehr, a Warners in-house editor.

Not predicting such a response – convinced, moreover, that the *THX 1138* cut would be considered a success by the studio – Coppola had brought with him to the screening seven more scripts for films Zoetrope wanted to make; these included those for *Apocalypse Now* and *The Conversation*. Yet Ted Ashley was so disturbed by *THX 1138* that he scrapped the Zoetrope deal – which meant that all the money invested, including that for making *THX 1138*, had to be paid back. George Lucas took upon his own shoulders the personal responsibility for the sunken Zoetrope dream; and as a counterpoint to this, a deep anger at Warners welled within him: the fact that ultimately only four minutes were cut from his film would do nothing to appease this huge internal rage at Hollywood's power-brokers. 'They were all interesting, adventurous scripts,' Lucas told journalist Stephen Farber. 'But then Warners decided not to finance any more youth-oriented, adventurous, crazy movies. They went back to hard-core entertainment films. For them it was a good decision, because they made a lot of money on that decision. But they sold us completely down the river.'

Eleven years later, as studios feverishly pitched for the release of *Raiders of the Lost Ark*, Ted Ashley would apologize to Lucas for having taken his picture away from him. Not that it helped him, for it was Paramount who put out *Raiders*, not Warners.

In fact, *THX 1138* was not a disaster: it brought Warner Brothers $945,000 in rentals. After the success of *Star Wars*, the film was re-released, with the cut footage restored. The film also earned Lucas a cult following in France, where it was a hit.

Struggling against the studios in the late 1960s to put their personal visions on screen were various alumni of American film schools. One of these was a man called Gary Kurtz, another product of USC's film-making course, who was endeavouring to push ahead as a producer. Born in July 1940, as a child Kurtz would religiously attend Saturday morning picture shows: he would be fascinated by *Flash Gordon* and other cliff-hanger serials.

Later, Kurtz had gone to Vietnam as a marine film-maker. The horror he saw there forced a spiritual awakening. Introduced one day in Mill Valley to George Lucas, Kurtz felt he had met someone he understood to be a fellow traveller.

Not long after, Lucas called him up to see if he was interested in working on a movie about Vietnam and the media circus that he was trying to get off the ground, to be called *Apocalypse Now*.

Since he had been at USC, Lucas had wanted to make a movie about the Vietnam War. He and John Milius, the gung-ho writer and later director, talked about it a lot: 'Surfing and bombs', they decided, was to be the main theme. Although Milius thought the film should be based on a helicopter journey, Lucas decided it should be a boat ride upriver. But this was long before any reference was made to Joseph Conrad's *Heart of Darkness*.

Investigating relevant source material, Lucas and Kurtz were taken with Kurosawa's 1958 classic *Hidden Fortress*. This is the story of a samurai leading a stroppy princess across wild enemy territory. The eventual central story of the first *Star Wars* draft bore a considerable resemblance to it.

The conflict in Vietnam was still raging, however, and Hollywood was unhappy about using an unconcluded war as subject-matter; among the studios there was no enthusiasm whatsoever for the project.

3 American Graffiti

Needing a paying gig, George Lucas filmed the 1969 Rolling Stones show at the Altamont Speedway for the Maysles brothers: they were making the documentary that became *Gimme Shelter*, the title being that of a song that was part of the group's repertoire. It could even have been Lucas who shot the footage of a fan being stabbed to death by a Hell's Angel, a recurring sequence in the film. The concert was considered a cultural watershed, the anti-Woodstock, as much a signifier of the end of the Sixties as the break-up of the Beatles the next year. Surely it must have had an immense impact on Lucas? Hardly at all – and as to whether or not he shot the footage of the killing, he simply doesn't know.

Besides, a different era of rock 'n' roll was starting to seep out from where it had logged itself away in his soul. What he wanted to do was make a film that was far from the futuristic world of his first feature. He would go back in time, rather than forward: specifically, he would make a movie about the world of cruising that had nearly ended his life. In doing so, Lucas continued the precedent begun with *THX 1138*: none of his films has ever been placed in the present-day.

Concerned with what he considered to be his personal weakness at story-telling, Lucas decided to let the narrative of his next film be driven by rock 'n' roll music of the late 1950s and early 1960s. And he would call the movie *American Graffiti*. The picture would be set during one hot summer's night in 1962 (the year Lucas graduated from college), when the lives of a group of young men interlaced and their futures became set in stone. The date was significant: this was the year prior to the assassination of President John F. Kennedy, marking the end of innocence in the United States.

But wouldn't he need more than one idea to attract studios? Feeling he needed a second carrot to dangle, George Lucas went forward in time again: always having loved the swashbuckling cliff-hanger *Flash Gordon* and *Buck Rogers* space serials he would watch on television as a child, he made an abortive attempt to purchase the rights to Alex Raymond's *Flash Gordon* books – but these already had been optioned by Federico Fellini.

I loved the *Flash Gordon* comic books [Lucas told *American Film*]. I loved the Universal serials with Buster Crabbe. After *THX 1138* I wanted to do *Flash Gordon* and tried to buy the rights to it from King Features, but they wanted a lot of money for it, more than I could afford then. They didn't really want to part with the rights – they wanted Fellini to do *Flash Gordon*.

I realized that I could make up a character as easily as Alex Raymond, who took his character from Edgar Rice Burroughs. It's your basic super-hero in outer space. I realized that what I really wanted to do was a contemporary action fantasy.

Knowing he needed to take another tack, Lucas decided instead to immerse himself in deep research into mythology.

The script for *American Graffiti* was initially developed for United Artists: they thought the project was too risky and dropped it. A year later, with the help of his recently acquired agent, Jeff Berg at Creative Management, Lucas pinned Universal down to a deal on the film. Lucas had refused to abandon the project.

> We were in dire financial straits, but I spent a year of my life trying to get that film off the ground. I was offered about three other pictures during that time. They all turned out to be duds. One of them was released at the same time as *Graffiti* – it's called *Lady Ice*. I turned that down at the bleakest point, when I was in debt to my parents, in debt to Francis Coppola, in debt to my agent; I was so far in debt I thought I'd never get out. Everybody in Hollywood had turned down *American Graffiti*. Universal had already turned it down once. And they offered me $75,000 to do *Lady Ice*, which is more money than I'd made in my entire life. And I said no. I said, 'By God, I've got a movie here, and I'm going to get it made somehow.' And I did.

Lucas had worked on the treatment and on the screenplay with Willard Huyck, whom he had met at USC, and Huyck's wife Gloria Katz, a graduate of the UCLA film course. 'I'm really quite lazy and I hate to write,' Lucas told Stephen Farber. 'Bill and Gloria added a lot of very witty dialogue and wrote all the scenes that I couldn't find my way to write. In my script, the characters of Steve and Laurie didn't work at all, and I couldn't make them work. The Huycks saved that. And they brought a lot of character to the hoods. My screenplay was much more realistic, and they added a lot more humour and fantasy to it, and improved it a great deal.'

The Universal contract partially hinged on the big guns that Lucas could bring to the table: specifically, Francis Ford Coppola, whose *The Godfather* had recently opened, immediately becoming an enormous hit that was also considered a deeply credible piece of art. For Universal, Coppola's name was an added fillip – they could already see the poster strapline: 'Produced by the director of *The Godfather*. . .' 'Francis was giving me a hard time too, and kept telling me to make something "warm and human" to prove I wasn't a cold guy. "You want warm and human?" I said, "All right, I'll give it to you." And I wrote *American Graffiti*.'

With his Zoetrope partner as part of the package, Lucas sold Universal on the idea. The studio agreed to finance and distribute *American Graffiti* – though they hated the title, suggesting instead that the film be called *Another Slow Night in Modesto* – an aberration that was defiantly resisted. The film was budgeted, however, at only $600,000, peanuts even by the standards of the time; later Jeff Berg managed to up the figure to $750,000.

Universal insisted, moreover, that this figure include all the music rights, which Columbia, who had passed on the film, had estimated could alone cost $500,000. In the end, the music cost only $90,000 for forty-five songs, thanks to a 'favoured nation' precedent-setting deal that Gary Kurtz managed to strike through his friend Dennis Wilson of the Beach Boys for the group's songs 'All Summer Long' and 'Surfin' Safari'. ('The Beach Boys were the only rock group who actually chronicled an era,' said Lucas. 'The blonde in the T-bird is from "Fun, Fun, Fun". "I Get Around" is about cruising . . . "Little Deuce Coupe" could be about John and his deuce coupe. "All Summer Long" – which is sort of the theme song of the film – talks about T-shirts and spilling Coke on your blouse . . . I always loved the Beach Boys because when we'd cruise, we'd listen to their songs, and it was as if the song was about us and what we were doing.')

Spurred on by the Universal deal, Lucas decided to rewrite the *American Graffiti* script himself. As he did so, he had his old records playing constantly, and this soundtrack to his writing shows: the film has the rhythm and energy of great early rock 'n' roll 45s. When George and Marcia Lucas cut the film together, each scene was set over the soundtrack of yet another rock 'n' roll classic. 'All good rock 'n' roll is classic teenage stuff, and all the scenes were such classic teenage scenes that they just sort of meshed, no matter how you threw them together. Sometimes even the words were identical. The most incredible example – and it was completely accidental – is in the scene where Steve and Laurie are dancing to "Smoke Gets in Your Eyes" at the sock hop, and at the exact moment where the song is saying "Tears I cannot hide", she backs off, and he sees that she's crying.'

The songs were tied together with the introductions and back-announcements of Wolfman Jack, the legendary disc jockey who broadcast rock 'n' roll to the entire United States from XERB, a radio station based in Mexico. ('When I was at USC, I made a documentary about a disc jockey. The idea behind it was radio as fantasy. For teenagers the person closest to them is a fantasy character. That's the disc jockey.')

Lucas himself had listened to Wolfman Jack when he was growing up in Modesto in the late Fifties and early Sixties. 'When we were cruising we could get Wolfman Jack from Tijuana. He was a really mystical character, I'll tell you. He was wild, he had these crazy phone calls, and he drifted out of nowhere. And it was such an outlaw station. He was an outlaw, which of course made him extremely attractive to kids.'

American Graffiti had a depth of feeling entirely missing in *THX 1138*; what is ostensibly a lightweight film has an extremely serious heart. Lucas was aware of this: he had become warm and positive, and it was as though his success came as some karmic consequence of that.

'After I finished *THX*,' he admitted to Stephen Farber, 'I was considered a cold, weird director, a science-fiction sort of guy who carried a calculator. And I'm not like that at all. So I thought, maybe I'll do something exactly the opposite. If they want warm human comedy, I'll give them one, just to show that I can do it. *THX* is very much the way that I am as a film-maker. *American Graffiti* is very much the way I am as a person – two different worlds really.'

The simplicity of *American Graffiti* was its strength. And the fact that it dealt with an Everyman reality: young people dangling on the cusp between teenagerdom and adulthood. The plot had four simple, cross-cutting storylines. Curt and Steve are to fly east to college in the morning. Steve, the super-straight class president, dates Laurie, the head cheerleader. Curt, sensitive and introspective, is having second thoughts about leaving a town that means more to him than he had realized. Thinking over his future, Curt searches for a mysterious woman in a Ford Thunderbird who has mouthed an enticement to him. Meanwhile, he is harassed by a duck-tailed gang called the Pharoahs. His indecision about leaving town cloaks the decision they must all meet: how to leave their world of childhood dreams.

Two other local teenagers get into further predicaments that are close to tragi-comic and deeply revealing. John, who rules the local drag strip, models himself on James Dean and drives the meanest deuce coupe in the valley, finds himself tricked into chaperoning twelve-year-old Carol. Terry the Toad is a nerd-like kid who rides only a Vespa scooter but finally gets a chance to play the stud: enticing a blonde bimbo called Debbie into the car that Steve has lent him, he then becomes anxious to hang on to her.

Only Curt and Steve have the option of leaving town and going to college. But after a car crash from which she emerges miraculously unscathed, Laurie throws herself into Steve's arms and begs him not to leave her. A decision made in the heat of emotion and insecurity seals his fate – Steve abandons his plan to leave town and go to college so that he can stay at home with his girl. Curt is the only one to climb aboard a plane out of the town in the morning – the only one to break free. Steve sees him off.

Although *THX 1138* had been impressive technically, the movie felt dry, even laboured, and it was clearly an effort to feel sympathy for its characters. Yet *THX* and *American Graffiti* have similar themes: *THX*, which is essentially a rewrite of George Orwell's 1984, describes how an individual breaks out of a spiritually deracinated, controlled world; *American Graffiti* also ends with one of the teenage boys breaking out of his background and escaping its cocoon.

'I've always been interested in that theme of leaving an environment or facing change, and how kids do it,' admitted Lucas. 'When I was eighteen or nineteen, I didn't know what I was going to do with my life. Where was I going to go, now that I was more or less free? What was I going to become? You can do anything you want at that age. And the kids who don't believe that are wrong. Both *THX* and *American Graffiti* are saying the same thing, that you don't have to do anything; it still is a free country.'

Beyond *American Graffiti*'s clearly autobiographical impulses, the film reflects Lucas's interest in sociology and anthropology: 'When I was in junior college, my primary major was in social sciences. I'm very interested in America and why it is what it is. I was always fascinated by the cultural phenomenon of cruising, that whole teenage mating ritual. It's really more interesting than primitive Africa or ancient New Guinea – and much, much weirder.'

Many of the events that take place in the film, said Lucas, 'are things that I actually experienced one way or another. They've also been fantasized, as they should be in a movie. They aren't really the way they were but the way they should have been.'

The film is filled with vignettes so familiar they are almost embarrassing.

I started out when I was young as Terry the Toad, and I think everybody starts out as Terry the Toad [Lucas told Stephen Farber]. And I went from that to being John; I had a hot car, and I raced around a lot. Finally I got into a very bad accident and almost got myself killed, and I spent a lot of time in the hospital. While I was in the hospital, I became much more academic-minded. I had been working as a mechanic, and I decided to give up cars and go to junior college, to try to get my grades back. So for the next two years, while I was at junior college, I more or less was Curt. I was thinking about leaving town, and I had a lot more perspective on things.'

But who was going to play these sharply drawn characters? At Haskell Wexler's commercials studio in Hollywood Lucas videotaped a shortlist of actors. In retrospect, the final line-up can be seen as a cast of extraordinary prescience. Among the actors *American Graffiti* introduced were Harrison Ford, Richard Dreyfuss (who played Curt), Ron Howard (Steve), twelve-year-old Mackenzie Phillips (the daughter of John and Michelle Phillips of The Mamas and The Papas group, who took the part of Carol), Cindy Williams (Laurie), Kathleen Quinlan, Kay Lenz, Suzanne Somers, Charles Martin Smith (Terry the Toad), Bo Hopkins, Candy Clark, and Paul LeMat (John the Cruising King).

As became an established part of his own mythology, Harrison Ford was largely making a living as a carpenter in the Hollywood area. New Yorker Dreyfuss, who had yet to appear in a movie, was initially offered the choice of playing either Curt or Toad. Paul LeMat, who plays the iconic John, a cigarette pack stuffed up the rolled sleeve of his T-shirt, had been a professional boxer. As for Ron Howard, although he was by now eighteen, he still carried his 'child actor' mantle – for years he had played Opie on *The Andy Griffith Show*.

What these soon-to-be stars were as yet unaware of, of course, was that each of the main actors was playing a part of George Lucas.

Filming on *American Graffiti* started on 26 June 1972. Lucas had just twenty-eight days to complete production, all of which would be a night shoot, on home ground in Marin County. 'We'd start at nine at night and end at five in the morning. In a regular movie, if you don't get what you're supposed to shoot one day, you can just throw up a few arc

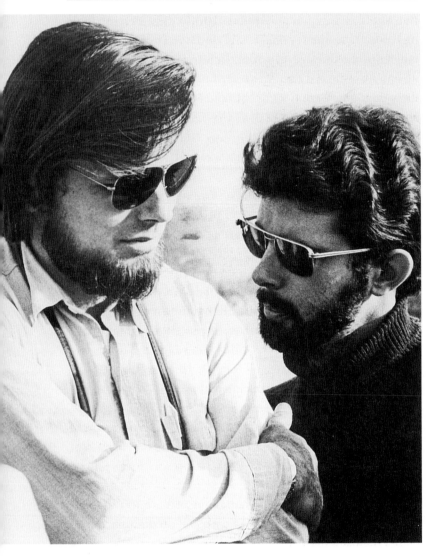

Gary Kurtz, co-producer with Francis Coppola of American Graffiti**, confers with Lucas on the set.**

lights and shoot for another hour. On *Graffiti*, when the sun came up, that was the end of the ballgame. We couldn't get one more shot. It was very hard on the crew. Nobody gets any sleep, so everybody's cranky. And it was very cold – like forty degrees. We had to shoot it in twenty-eight days, and sometimes we'd do as many as thirty set-ups in one night. So we had a horrendous problem.'

Things did not begin very auspiciously: the day before shooting began, a crew member was busted for possession of marijuana – although, as *Graffiti* was a 'youth' movie, this might well have been considered a positive omen.

But there were to be more difficulties. Night one was to be shot in San Rafael, a small town near where Lucas lived in Mill Valley. But the director could not get the cameras up on to the cars – his first shot was not filmed until 2 a.m.

Most of the scenes were set to be shot in San Rafael. On the second night, however, the cast and crew turned up only to be told that their filming permit had been revoked after a local bar claimed to have lost business the previous evening. A temporary truce was struck under which filming could continue in San Rafael for a further three nights. Then the production would shift to Petaluma, twenty miles to the north.

But the hassles of the second night had not yet ended: first the streets were blocked by traffic after fire ravaged a restaurant; then Barney Coangelo, the assistant cameraman, slipped and was run over by the car he was filming.

George Lucas began to be worried. And there was more to come: the cameramen he had hired had minimal feature-film experience and he quickly learned that they couldn't come up with what he wanted. Accordingly, Lucas turned to his old friend Haskell Wexler for help. There was no money left in the budget, so instead Lucas offered Wexler a point of the film's profits to take over as cinematographer – a deal that turned out to be extremely lucrative.

Each night Wexler would arrive in Petaluma from Los Angeles, where he would spend the days shooting advertisements. Then he would film *American Graffiti* all night. Wexler demonstrated that he thoroughly deserved his title of lighting cameraman: to create the neon Wurlitzer jukebox look that Lucas sought for the movie, for example, he taped soft glowing lights all over the inside of the car roofs.

'He's really, in my estimation, the best cameraman in this country,' said Lucas. 'Essentially he was working in a medium he hated – widescreen. He hated Technoscope because it's very grainy and doesn't look very good. I wanted the film to look sort of like a Sam Kartzman beach-party movie, all yellow and red and orange. And Haskell figured out how to do it. He devised what he calls jukebox lighting . . . The movie looked exactly the way I wanted it to look – very much like a carnival.'

In *American Graffiti* there were plenty of knowing in-jokes: the local movie theatre, for example, is showing *Dementia 13*, Coppola's first feature; and Milner's deuce coupe carries the licence plate *THX 1138*. In scene one a girl parks an Edsel at Mel's Drive-in.

Although Lucas wanted his wife Marcia to cut *American Graffiti*, Universal insisted on someone with more experience. The studio was pleased with the work of Lucas's former employer Verna Fields on *Sugarland Express*, a film by Steven Spielberg, another young director. The prospect of working with her again stimulated Lucas, and in ten weeks Fields took the film to rough-cut stage.

At 10 a.m. on Sunday 28 January 1973 at San Francisco's Northpoint Theater, *American Graffiti* was previewed for the first time. What followed was extraordinary: Ned Tanen, representing Universal, was in a bad mood: on the flight from Los Angeles he had refused to sit with others on their way to the preview. After the film ended, to an ecstatic response from the eight hundred-strong audience, Tanen immediately left the venue, stepping out into the street with Gary Kurtz. He was apoplectic with anger. 'This is in no shape to show to an audience. It's unreleasable,' he raged.

Then he returned to the theatre, almost immediately running into Francis Coppola. The team making the film had let him down, he snapped. George Lucas heard what the studio executive said and immediately went into deep shock, fearing a repeat of his *THX 1138* experiences.

Coppola fought back on the spot, not mincing words. In front of the departing audience, he let Tanen know precisely what he thought: 'You should get down on your knees and thank George for saving your job. This kid has killed himself to make this movie for you.' Then he delivered a long lecture to Tanen, berating him for his insensitivity towards Lucas, and ending with an offer to buy the film from Universal. 'This movie's going to be a hit! The audience loved this movie! I saw it with my own eyes!' he told Tanen.

At a further meeting in San Francisco the next day Tanen was mollified. He still insisted, however, on several changes. Lucas was infuriated by this: again, a movie he had made was being taken away from him. But a compromise was

arrived at, and Lucas set out to make the changes himself.
After the director had spent a month recutting and remixing
the film, Tanen was still dissatisfied. Lucas, Coppola and
Kurtz came to the conclusion that they should ask Verna
Fields to rejoin the film, operating as a buffer between themselves and Universal. Ultimately, the cuts only amounted to
four and a half minutes of footage.

Yet again Lucas considered himself to have been mortally
betrayed by the studio. Like the characters in his subsequent
films, he only saw life as good and bad, light and dark;
rightly or wrongly, there were no shades of grey in George
Lucas's life.

Tanen scheduled another screening for 15 May 1973, at the
Writers' Guild Theater in Beverly Hills.

Operating as what would be known nowadays as a spin-
doctor, Gary Kurtz worked to ensure that *Graffiti* would only be
shown to Universal executives when they were counterbal-
anced by the company of an appropriately youthful audience.
At Kurtz's request Wolfman Jack packed the place with kids;
most of the film's stars also attended. The film was a huge hit;
Steven Spielberg considered it the most powerful screening he
had ever attended.

American Graffiti opened on 1 August 1973. That evening,
Cindy Williams happened to drive past the Avco Cinema in
the Westwood section of Los Angeles, an area with a large
student population. She was astonished at what she saw. 'I
never thought I'd be in a movie with lines around the block,'
she told friends in amazement.

The film was an enormous hit, the most profitable film
investment that its Hollywood studio had ever made. It cost

$775,000 and sold $117 million in tickets, making it the highest cost-to-profit ratio film Fox had ever had. It simply ran for ever.

With the success of *American Graffiti*, Lucas had shown he was adept at tapping into and understanding the cutting edge of the *zeitgeist*. Despite its skilful 'Where Were You In '62?' poster, *American Graffiti* was a film that was resolutely about the 1950s and rock 'n' roll, even if from time to time it commented on them ironically. In fact, it helped spur the first flood of nostalgia for the era. *Happy Days*, which appeared shortly afterwards, was a television version of *American Graffiti*, with Ron Howard re-working his film role. *Grease*, *That'll Be the Day*, *Hot Wax* and biopics of Elvis Presley (by John Carpenter) and Buddy Holly (starring Gary Busey) would soon follow.

'In a way the film was made so my father won't think those were wasted years,' Lucas confided to Stephen Farber, referring to his teenage cruising lifestyle. 'I can say I was doing research, though I didn't know it at the time.'

But what was George Lucas going to do next? The director was in debt to the tune of $15,000: the money from *Graffiti* had not yet come in. He knew he had to start repaying his debts.

And so, sufficiently inspired, he set about the research for *Star Wars*.

4 Star Wars

When the *American Graffiti* money was freed up, it poured into Lucas's bank account as though from an open tap – his promise to his father that he would be a millionaire by the time he was thirty had been easily achieved. This did not make Francis Ford Coppola happy, however: had he financed *American Graffiti* himself, he would have made $30 million on the deal. But wasn't the perspective of George Lucas more sound? 'I had never been interested in making money, just in making movies. I became rich and successful by accident. The only thing I worried about was that the studio might lose money. As long as the film broke even, I felt I had done my job. Believe me, I did not set out to make a blockbuster movie with *Graffiti*.' The success unleashed a subtext between the two film-makers, in which each suspected the other of wanting to dominate him.

When the 1973 Academy Awards were announced, *American Graffiti* had been nominated for several Oscars: those for Best Picture, Best Direction, Best Original Screenplay (the Huycks and Lucas), Best Supporting Actress and Best Film Editing. In the end, it did not win any of these, the Paul Newman and Robert Redford vehicle *The*

Sting sweeping the awards that year. *American Graffiti* ended up with the consolation prize of a Golden Globe for Best Comedy Picture of the Year.

What was George Lucas to do with his new-found wealth? In an unprecedented gesture, he gave quite a lot of it away to people who had worked on the film. Several individuals who had been given points on the film became millionaires. The principal cast members had one point split ten ways between them. Richard Dreyfuss, for example, had been paid $5,000 to make the film, but received an additional $70,000. Haskell Wexler got his one point – then Coppola gave him two more: Wexler made almost a million dollars from a job that had literally been moonlighting.

As well as *Star Wars*, George Lucas had other eggs in the basket. *Apocalypse Now* had been one of the Zoetrope projects dumped by Warner Brothers. But Coppola had paid back the development money out of his *Godfather* profits, which meant he owned the screenplays.

Yet Lucas still wanted to make *Apocalypse Now* himself. After finishing *American Graffiti*, he struck a development deal for the Vietnam film with Columbia. He wanted the film to be cheap, with a budget of under $2 million, using 16mm cameras. Lucas and John Milius worked on a screenplay that they soon completed. Gary Kurtz went location-scouting in the Philippines.

George Lucas was partly hedging his bets, because he had become doubtful about his ability to get *Star Wars* into shape, having identified the colossal weight of research and writing that was going to be involved. *Apocalypse Now* seemed to be the next logical film to make. But the subject-matter of

Apocalypse Now was beginning to cause an internal conflict: *American Graffiti* had provided a powerful lesson: 'I discovered that making positive films is exhilarating.' And Coppola was insisting that because of the previous Zoetrope deal, he would take twenty-five per cent of the profits as producer if Lucas did make the Vietnam picture; while Lucas would have to split his twenty-five per cent with Milius. Lucas smarted at this – and went back to work on *Star Wars*.

A man of personal integrity, Lucas was disturbed that the studios had cut a few minutes from both *THX 1138* and *American Graffiti*. But he anticipated more battles with studios:

> Every time you have a successful film, you do get a few more things in your contract. The film I'm writing now, *The Star Wars*, has been turned down by a couple of studios already, but now we're finally getting a deal because they say, 'Oh, he's had a hit movie. We don't really know about the idea, but he's a hot director, so let's do it.' They don't do it on the basis of the material: they do it on the kind of deal they can make, because most of the people at the studios are former agents, and all they know are deals. They're like used-car dealers.

He also sensed that audiences were tiring of the grittier, bloody new cinema. 'You can learn from cynicism, but you can't build on it,' Lucas said to the *Los Angeles Times* in 1973.

In 1974 Coppola tried again with Lucas: he told him he thought they could do even better with *Apocalypse Now* than they had with *American Graffiti*. Lucas told Coppola he was ploughing ahead with *Star Wars*. All the same, he admitted that he still did really want to make the Vietnam picture and asked Coppola to wait until *Star Wars* was finished. By now, however, Coppola was insisting that *Apocalypse Now* should come out in 1976, the US bi-centennial year.

In the end, the making of *Apocalypse Now*, with Coppola as director, took more than two years – it came nowhere near that 1976 release date. And it nearly finished Coppola, who did all the same give Lucas two production points. For his own part, Lucas had been shocked that Coppola would not wait for him to direct the film, in which he had invested six years of his life. When Coppola finally completed *Apocalypse Now*, it contained a brief scene in which Harrison Ford appeared. As Coppola zooms in on his shirt, the name tag can be clearly read: Col. G. Lucas.

Then matters took a further twist: Lucas had closed a deal for *Star Wars* with Fox. Alan Ladd Jr., a Fox production executive and son of the film star, had talent-spotted him at the time of *THX 1138*, admiring his directing and vision. Meeting him, he had also been impressed by Lucas's honesty and professionalism – and he was extremely taken with *American Graffiti*.

Ladd had a reputation for creating a warm, congenial work atmosphere, conducive to the flow of creativity. One of the filmmakers he supported was Mel Brooks: Warners had refused to release *Blazing Saddles* until Ladd scooped it up for Fox.

At a further meeting Ladd failed to grasp Lucas's concept of *Star Wars*.

As a kid I read a lot of science fiction [Lucas told Stephen Zito in *American Film*]. But instead of reading technical, hard-science writers like Isaac Asimov, I was interested in Harry

Harrison and fantastic, surreal approaches to the genre. I grew up on it. *Star Wars* is a sort of compilation of this stuff, but it's never been put in one story before, never put down on film. There is a lot taken from western, mythology, and samurai movies. It's all the things that are great put together. It's not like one kind of ice-cream but rather a very big sundae . . . It's very surreal and bizarre and has nothing to do with science. I wanted it to be an adventure in space, like *John Carter on Mars*. That was before science took over, and everything got very serious and science oriented.

Star Wars has more to do with disclaiming science than anything else. There are very elaborate, Rube Goldberg explanations for things. It's a totally different galaxy with a totally different way of thinking. It's not based on science, which bogs you down. I don't want the movie to be about anything that would happen or be real. I wanted to tell a fantasy story.

Lucas sold *Star Wars* to Ladd as being a blend of *Buck Rogers*, *Captain Blood* and *The Sea Hawk*: the director said that the idea of the film was 'a subtle suggestion that opening the door and going out there, no matter what the risk, is sometimes worth the effort'. Though Ladd didn't quite get what Lucas meant, he expressed his desire to link up with him on the project.

His chance soon came. Although Universal had released *American Graffiti*, they passed on giving Lucas the $25,000 he asked for to turn his *Star Wars* treatment into a script. Had they done so, the studio would have made $250 million.

The day after Universal turned Lucas down on *Star Wars*, Ladd said he'd give Lucas $50,000 to write the film and $250,000 to direct it. Furthermore, forty per cent of the net profits would go to the Star Wars Corporation, a company Lucas had created. Lucas, meanwhile, would retain rights of control over *Star Wars*; especially over its merchandising (Lucas was to receive fifty per cent of every merchandising deal that Fox struck for *Star Wars*), soundtrack and – most importantly – sequel rights. Extraordinarily, Fox signed a deal with Lucas without demanding sequel rights.

Although the initial budget was set at $2.5 million, Lucas knew that the film would cost much more: he was trying to keep Ladd locked into the deal. This in turn took time to put together. By November 1975, Lucas had spent most of his first $1 million chunk of *American Graffiti* profits on *Star Wars* pre-production.

The Making of *Star Wars*

The birth of cinema coincided approximately with that of flight. Since George Melies made *A Trip to the Moon* in 1902, science fiction had proved an enduringly appealing theme, one to which Hollywood periodically applied itself. In the 1950s there had been a burst of films – *Invasion of the Body Snatchers*, *It Came from Outer Space*, *Forbidden Planet*, *The Day the Earth Stood Still* amongst others – that were seen as metaphors for the Cold War. The last significant cinematic piece of science fiction had been Kubrick's *2001: A Space Odyssey*, in 1968 – despite huge critical acclaim, the revered film had been tardy in earning back its budget.

In post-war children's fantasies, spacemen had always run a distinct second to cowboys, the stars of Hollywood's far more successful genre, the western. However, westerns had fallen out of favour with the studios after television had turned out an enormous number of cowboy series; they had also gone through considerable revision in order to accommodate the era's shifting cultural positions, especially towards native Americans.

So there had been a switch: new kinds of cowboys were needed, ones who could exist in the expanded consciousness of inner and outer space. And to find them, why not go back to the traditional Hollywood values of humour and adventure films?

> I wanted to do a modern fairy-tale, a myth [George Lucas told Stephen Zito in *American Film*]. One of the criteria of the mythical fairy-tale situation is an exotic, faraway land, but we've lost all the fairy-tale lands on this planet. Every one has disappeared. We no longer have the Mysterious East or treasure islands or going on strange adventures.
>
> But there is a bigger, mysterious world in space that is more interesting than anything around here. We've just begun to take the first step and can say, 'Look! It goes on for a zillion miles out there.' You can go anywhere and land on any planet.

Since finishing *American Graffiti*, Lucas had worked assiduously. That film, he told David Sheff in *Rolling Stone* in 1987, had been about

> the fact that you can't hang on to the past. The future may be completely strange and different and scary, but that's the way it should be. I thought that was one of the biggest challenges facing teenagers. I got to do what I wanted to do by not being frightened by the future and the unknown, and I figured that was a good message to get across. *Star Wars* says the same thing in terms of technology, space flight and opening up the world.

. . . The idea is not to be afraid of change. There are bad robots, good robots, aliens and monsters in all forms. *Star Wars* shows progression. You may be frightened – and it's sad because you are leaving something behind – but go forward. That's what life is about. You can either have a good attitude about change or a bad attitude about it. You can't fight tidal waves, you can only ride them. So the best thing to do is get your surfboard and make the best of it.

Now for his next movie he researched mythology and social psychology, 'studying the pure form to see how and why it worked. When I did *Star Wars*, I consciously tried to find age-old themes. I think of mythology as archaeology of the mind,' he said later.

Lucas hated writing. Every sentence was dragged out of him. 'Three hours writing and five hours thinking' was how he defined his work method. Scissors were kept on his desk: in a haze of neurotic frustration, he would snip away at his hair and beard.

But he took notes constantly, which paid off all the time. Once, while out with a disc jockey friend, Terry McGovern, the DJ's car bumped over a hole in the road. 'Must have run over a wookie back there,' ad-libbed McGovern, inventing a generic name. Meanwhile, Indiana, George and Marcia Lucas's black-and-white malamute, evolved into Chewbacca, Solo's partner. In his turn, the character of Han Solo was based on John Milius.

In the first treatment of the film George Lucas set the story in the twenty-third century: the Jedi-Templar warriors swore allegiance to the Alliance of Independent Systems. Jungle and desert planets, and a city suspended in the clouds were the three settings. Individuals, animals and areas were described in the most minute detail, becoming living entities.

The film's title mutated. *The Story of Mace Windu* became *Adventures of the Starkiller, Episode One of the Star Wars*, which evolved into simply *The Star Wars*. The script was now something like five hundred pages long, almost five times as long as was necessary. Then George Lucas divided the story up into three parts. After putting away two of these sections, to be later wrestled to the ground, he worked at honing the remainder into what finally became the first *Star Wars* film.

The central character, Luke Starkiller, worked on his uncle Owen Lars's farm on the desert planet of Tatooine. At this stage Lars was a clear character who had taken his nephew's money to set up his farm. Owen Lars knew the true identity of Luke's father, Anakin Starkiller.

Leia was a sixteen-year-old hostage of the Empire: Lucas resisted the entreaties of Coppola who wanted him to have a pre-pubescent young girl star as what evolved into the Princess Leia character. Obi-Wan Kenobi guarded the more arcane knowledge and wisdom of the Jedi knights and the Force, the notion of which came from the story in Carlos Castaneda's *Tales of Power* in which the Native American shaman, Don Juan, talked of a 'life force'.

Both Lucas and Gary Kurtz were extremely taken with the works of Carl Jung and the concept of archetypes. They were heavily influenced by Joseph Campbell's *Hero with a Thousand Faces*, his enlightening survey of world mythology: when, years later, Campbell filmed a series of television interviews, the shoot took place at Lucas's premises.

In fact, many of the stories and themes in *Star Wars* already had been selected by Joseph Campbell in *Hero with a Thousand Faces*. The Arthurian quest of the knight, for example, as well as the biblical renewal of faith, the struggle of man versus machine, and the notion of the Good and Bad father which became separated into the characters of Darth Vader and Obi-Wan Kenobi. Even the Jonah and the whale story becomes incorporated into the plot: in *The Empire Strikes Back*, the *Millennium Falcon* is swallowed whole by a monster.

The trilogy of films, in fact, is stitched together with so much cosmic symbolism that it becomes taken as a given: for example, both Yoda's swampland of the bog planet Dagobah and the barren wastelands of Tatooine symbolize aspects of the soul and the unconscious.

'All I was trying to say in a very simple and straightforward way is that there is a God and there is a good and bad side,' was how George Lucas explained away *Star Wars* later.

To do so, he created characters who were archetypes. Luke Skywalker, for example, is a traditional adolescent hero who undergoes a mythological-like rite of passage to manhood. His aunt and uncle having been tragically killed, he undertakes a mission against superhuman and supernatural odds, overcoming the threat of destruction and death.

The psychological and philosophical underpinning of the *Star Wars* trilogy was expressed through assorted gurus and the constant of the Force, as though Lucas had defined the deity as consisting of pure energy – again, a cutting-edge belief. The Force was an energy field created by all living things in the universe: after death, their energy was collected like a force in the sky into which the magician-warriors who comprised the Jedi knights were able to tap. The Force had both a dark and a light side, and with subtlety embodied the tenets of Christianity, Buddhism, Judaism and Islam, as well as more personal philosophies. 'The laws really are in yourself,' Lucas was fond of saying, and he later defined this intangible spirit: 'The Force is what happens in spite of us that we can either use or not use. We can fight these changes, or we can use them, incorporate them into our lives, take full advantage of them.'

The origins of some of the *Star Wars* characters, however, were mundane rather than arcane. The robots R2-D2 and C-3PO had the function of providing comic relief, like science-fiction versions of Laurel and Hardy. During the cutting of *American Graffiti*, Walter Murch had once asked George Lucas for R2, D2 (Reel 2, Dialogue 2) of the film. Lucas had liked the abbreviated sound, thinking it matched perfectly his notion of a 'cute' robot – the original inspiration for which had come from the robot in Douglas Trumbull's *Silent Running*.

As well as studying mythology, George Lucas made sure he understood his potential audience. Each weekend he would go out and buy up all the science-fiction magazines and comics he could find, telling Marcia he was trying to understand the minds of ten-year-old boys.

Lucas was plugged into a different culture from that of the studio executives. He knew how important it was, in helping create a word-of-mouth buzz, that he had done a deal with Marvel for a *Star Wars* comic.

Also, that he had cut a deal to have a *Star Wars* novelization published, as well as a book about the making of the film.

That *Star Wars* should not be sold as science fiction he also knew to be crucial: such a marketing campaign had damaged *THX 1138*. The paradox here is that the main influence on *Star Wars* is *THX 1138*: the robot police became stormtroopers; OMM is a benevolent version of the Emperor; the hunchbacked shell dwellers became Jawas; THX, the hero who escapes and faces the responsibilities of his new existence, became Luke Skywalker.

From the *Flash Gordon* serials he had loved, George Lucas took art deco sets, blaster guns, medieval costumes and video screens. And he took their constant action. Ming, the evil ruler of Mongo in the *Flash Gordon* books, became a model for Lucas' emperor. From *John Carter on Mars*, he took *Star Wars*' beasts of burden, the banthas. The library of old movies he devoured covered the spectrum from *Forbidden Planet* to *The Day the World Ended*.

Lucas found all this research, even all the meetings, quite palatable. But writing the script remained a nightmare. Writing in pencil in tiny cramped handwriting, using a number two hard lead pencil, Lucas had stomach and chest pains and constant headaches until the screenplay was finished.

As he wrote, the plot of *Star Wars* mutated. Originally the *Star Wars* hero had been a Jedi knight general. Lucas saw there could be more character change if Luke Skywalker was a young man who became a Jedi. The resulting character, moreover, was rooted in the dualism within Lucas: half innocent and idealistic naïf, half cynical pessimist. Eventually, the second aspect of this psychological make-up was removed to become Han Solo.

But as Luke's character grew, that of Princess Leia receded from her previously dominant stance: to maintain the interest of the audience she was given a love interest with Han Solo.

The first screenplay took a year to develop and was finished in May 1974. Screenplay two was finished on 28 January 1975. It had been given a title: *Adventures of the Starkiller, Episode One of the Star Wars*.

Version two was set in the Republica Galactica, a land torn by civil strife and banditry. Part of the plot involved a search for the Kiber Crystal, whose energy field was in charge of the destiny of all life.

Only Lucas understood the world he was creating, which had a total span of fifty-five years. For the time being he was to concentrate on the middle trilogy. The first trilogy would be set twenty years before *Star Wars*: its story was that of young Ben Kenobi and Luke's father. The final trilogy would tell the story of the adult Luke's final war between the Empire and the rebels. C-3PO and R2-D2 were the only constants common to all nine films.

This new version of *The Star Wars* continued to have two elements: a rescue mission to save a hostage taken by Darth Vader and the ensuing struggle to destroy the Death Star. The final air battle had been in the script from the onset of the writing, and Lucas felt obliged to contain it within the final script. But despite its technological bravura, in the finished film it can almost feel like an add-on. (By choosing the *Millennium Falcon* as the name of Han Solo's spaceship, Lucas had touched on the unconscious resonance of the present time as it shifts into the next thousand years, at the same time giving a timeless quality to the vessel.)

Version three of the screenplay was handed in on 1 August 1975. In it the Force was still symbolized by the Kiber

Crystal. But it was no longer there in version four, completed by the end of March 1976. This script still included Luke's older brother Biggs, who survived right through to the final shoot, only to be edited out of the final cut.

To help him secure his deal with Fox, Lucas initially had called on the work of Ralph McQuarrie, who had sketched the Apollo missions for CBS News and created the Boeing parts catalogue. He wanted the look of *Star Wars* to be, he told him, 'used space'.

McQuarrie was given the third version of the screenplay, as well as illustrations from *Flash Gordon* books and comic book examples. McQuarrie was commissioned to paint five scenes: these included a group portrait of the major characters and the final attack on the Death Star. As much as the paintings had sold the film to the studio, so they clarified Lucas's vision for him. McQuarrie, for example, thought that Darth Vader was insufficiently sinister when wearing black robes: he introduced the idea of the Lord of Darkness as a figure armoured in black. The colour was right, but the texture was still wrong: to the armour he added a black cloak.

Lucas took on board McQuarrie's suggestions of Chewbacca's look, but softened it – though leaving the trademark looping cartridge belts.

With the script and the look of the film in place, all that was needed was someone to play the characters.

A large cast had to be found. To reduce the stress of this task, Lucas made a pact with Brian de Palma, who was about to cast for *Carrie*, a Hitchcock pastiche. Together they looked

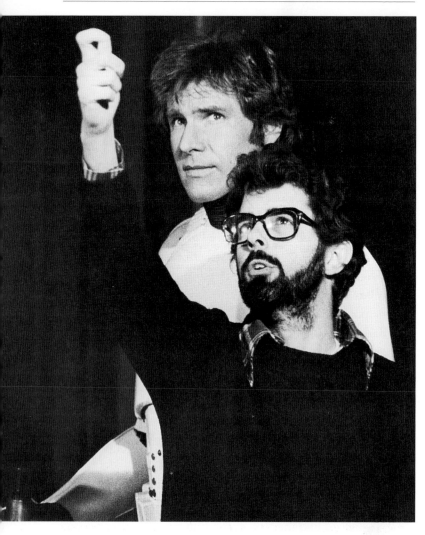

Harrison Ford's good looks as well as his fractious mood during the audition made him perfect for the part of Han Solo.

at the legions of prospective talent. Lucas kept firmly in the background: at Mark Hamill's audition he was sufficiently low-key for Hamill to imagine he must be de Palma's gofer.

Following his habitual financially astute path, Harrison Ford had gone back to his craft of carpentry after *American Graffiti* – this was partly because his *Graffiti* earnings had allowed him to buy such an expensive tool-set that he felt he ought to be employing it on tasks other than doing up his ramshackle home in the Hollywood hills. While the *Star Wars* auditions were taking place Ford was putting in a new door at Francis Coppola's offices. Although he knew of the casting, Ford had heard that Lucas had said he wouldn't be using any actors from *American Graffiti*. All the same, Lucas asked Ford if he wouldn't mind reading the male parts as he tried out actors for the role of Princess Leia. Ford complied, but grew testy as he began to realize he was reading parts which would not be his. Lucas, however, picked up that his fractious mood was ideal for the similarly argumentative Han Solo: physically rugged, Ford also projected a sly intelligence.

Finally Lucas had it narrowed it down to two groups of possibles: the first consisted of the New York stage actor Christopher Walken as Han Solo, television actor Will Selzer as Luke, former Penthouse Pet, Terri Nunn as Leia; and the second of Harrison Ford, Mark Hamill and Carrie Fisher, the eighteen-year-old daughter of Eddie Fisher and Debbie Reynolds. It may have been her showbiz aristocratic background that gave Fisher the sufficiently regal and imperious manner she brought to the part; she also seemed slightly asexual. Soon Lucas plumped for the second set of actors.

Harrison Ford was awkward about money. He was only being offered $1,000 a week to play Han Solo: he could make more than that in his carpentry business, he insisted. But Lucas wouldn't move. Accordingly, Ford refused to commit himself to a deal to appear in any sequels – as Hamill and Fisher already had agreed to do.

Lucas had always seen Obi-Wan 'Ben' Kenobi acted by someone of the stature of Sir Alec Guinness; and in 1975 he found Guinness in Los Angeles, filming the Neil Simon-scripted spoof thriller *Murder by Death*. Not only did Guinness go for the part – he had found the script compulsive reading – but he brought his own thoughts to it, assisting Lucas to understand the essential conflict between Obi-Wan Kenobi and Darth Vader.

Eventually George Lucas decided that if no one in Hollywood could offer him the special effects he wanted, he would build them from scratch. In Los Angeles he hired John Dykstra, a special effects assistant on *2001*, *The Andromeda Strain* and *Silent Running*, who had some experience of computer-controlled cameras.

Computer-controlled cameras were already changing television but so far had hardly been used in feature films. Dykstra was given the task of altering this. In July 1975 Lucasfilm Ltd created a subsidiary called Industrial Light and Magic, to be run by the special-effects wizard. Dykstra set about creating the computer system for the over 350 special effects in the film. The method he devised hinged around a giant camera mounted on tracks, powered by high-torque motors controlled by a computer. Each shot was programmed into a computer and played back a number of times to accommodate the model elements in the shots, creating the effect of live-action shots.

It was not until December 1975 that *Star Wars* was given the final green light by Fox. By then Lucas had poured a million of his own dollars into development. Since Lucas had first linked up with Alan Ladd, the budget had spiralled seemingly out of control.

When Lucas had first gone to Ladd, the director had said that the film would cost $3.5 million. Then Lucas and Gary Kurtz worked out what they considered to be the real budget – and found that it came to almost four times that much: $12 million. When that budget was shown to Ladd, he had pared it down to a figure of $8.5 million. Somewhere down the line Lucas put in a budget of $7.887 million – it became a running joke at Fox that the *Star Wars* budget was the same backwards or forwards.

Whatever, Lucas already knew he didn't have enough money. Moreover, until the budget was crisply finalized, Fox had wanted to stop all pre-production work. Armed with his *American Graffiti* cash cow, however, Lucas declared he would push on – even if it meant financing the movie himself. Which forced Fox to quicken its decision-making process.

The Shooting of *Star Wars*

Despite Fox having approved a final budget, it was imperative to keep costs down. Accordingly, Gary Kurtz made the economical choice to shoot the film in England, at Elstree, an hour's drive from central London: if *Star Wars* had been shot in the US and not Elstree it would have cost $13 million.

With shooting about to begin, much was still not quite ready. For example, Lucas asked Bill Huyck and Gloria Katz at the last minute to take the dialogue up another level, especially the smart-ass raps between Han Solo and Princess Leia. The pair were given percentage points on the film.

Industrial Light and Magic (ILM) were supposed to have come up with shots against which the action could be back-projected. But nothing was ready. Just before filming began, Lucas decided that instead he would blue-screen the action – they would film against a blank blue background and add the optical special effects in post-production.

And George Lucas had something else on his mind. He was endlessly undecided: should the hero of *Star Wars* be called Luke Starkiller or Luke Skywalker? It was not until the day before filming began that he came to a final decision.

Casting had continued when the production moved to London. Chewbacca was to be played by Peter Mayhew, a seven foot two inches tall London hospital porter, the possessor of one of the biggest pairs of feet in England.

In London Anthony Daniels had been chosen to play C-3PO, the robot that had all manner of resonations with the character of The Tin Man in *The Wizard of Oz*. For the making of C-3PO's mould, Daniels was stripped naked, his private parts protected with plastic film. Then he was covered in Vaseline and coated from head to toe in plaster.

Sir Alec Guinness had needs of a different sort. Specifically, this grand old man of the English stage and cinema required a five-figure cheque. And he also took two and a quarter per cent of the gross profits of *Star Wars*. Guinness would make more money from *Star Wars* than from any other film that he had appeared in.

Shooting was not to begin in Elstree, but in the hospitable North African country of Tunisia. On the edge of the Sahara desert they had found ideal territory to represent the arid wastelands of Tatooine.

Day one of the *Star Wars* shoot, 26 March 1976, was reminiscent of the disaster-strewn first night of filming on *American Graffiti*. The day after the production crew and cast had set up in the tiny desert town of Chott el-Djerid it rained for the first time in fifty years. The parched landscape was transformed into an ocean of mud.

When filming finally got under way, the crew were struck by the beauty of C-3PO, this golden man illuminated by the glare of the desert sun. But being trapped inside the robot's body for twelve hours a day in the desert heat was torture for Anthony Daniels.

Fortunately for the future of the film, an instant empathy sparked between Mark Hamill and Sir Alec Guinness; they struck up a friendship that showed on the screen. Guinness already had been through a not inconsiderable crisis. For Lucas had made a significant script change: Obi-Wan Kenobi, he had decided, would die in a duel with Darth Vader. Then he would reappear as a spirit guide, thereby becaming the personification of the Force. Disturbed by this script-change, Guinness had threatened to withdraw from the production before Lucas won him over.

While in Tunisia, Hamill tried a pass at a scene by playing it precisely as he imagined Lucas himself would respond in similar circumstances. 'Perfect,' assessed the director. Ah, thought Mark Hamill, so Luke Skywalker *is* George Lucas. But he also noticed that at no point did Lucas come and talk to him about his character. Although this was

characteristic of Lucas, he was all the same taken with
Hamill's innocence.

In retrospect, the desert conditions of Tunisia were clearly a
pointer to future climatic conditions on the production: 1976
was to be Britain's then hottest summer of the twentieth
century. Even inside the normally cool sound stages, Elstree
was sweltering.

And George Lucas himself was to become particularly
hot under the collar when he learned that, in the British
film business, nothing comes without its price. Never
having previously worked in Britain, the director was
enraged to discover that the solidly unionized British
film crews refused to work past 5.30 in the afternoon.
When Lucas proposed that they stay for an extra two hours'
shooting each night, the suggestion was resoundingly
defeated in a union ballot.

'George wasn't happy there – he doesn't like to be away
from home,' admitted Gary Kurtz. 'There are a lot of little
things that are bothersome – light switches go up instead of
down. Everything is different enough to throw you off. . . All
film crews are a matter of chemistry. George is not a particularly social person. He doesn't go out of his way to socialize.
It takes him a while to know somebody, to get intimate enough
to share his problems with them. It's easier for him to work
with people he knows.'

Notwithstanding the weather, Lucas was sickly throughout
the shoot, with assorted stress-related colds and flus. And
only he really knew what he wanted the film to be, which
immediately put him at odds with his cinematographer,
Gilbert 'Gil' Taylor, an E-type Jaguar-driving, gentleman

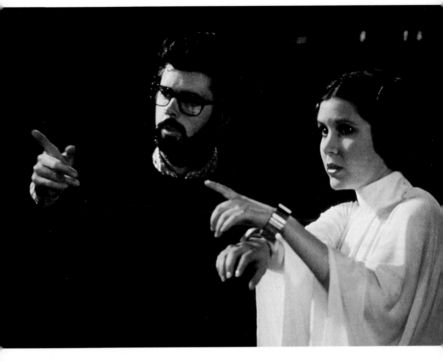

During the filming of Star Wars**, Fisher became the target of Lucas' sometimes hectoring manner – 'Stand up, be a princess!' she would be told.**

farmer who had filmed Richard Lester's *A Hard Day's Night*,
Stanley Kubrick's *Dr Strangelove*, and Alfred Hitchcock's
Frenzy. Taylor had few problems with Lucas's work method,
however: quickly he learned that Lucas likes to shoot fast –
going for it, getting the adrenalin racing. With a clear view
of how his story-boarded scene would look in the cutting-
room, he would rarely film more than four or five takes; he
showed an instinctive understanding of how to move and
pace a film, notably when integrating the three big set-piece
situations in each of the *Star Wars* films.

Alfed Hitchcock had directed his first films at Elstree in
Borehamwood – 'Boring Wood', as Harrison Ford renamed it.
Often it seemed as though Lucas was going along with
Hitchcock's apocryphal opinion that actors were no better
than cattle: from time to time Carrie Fisher would become
the target of Lucas' sometimes hectoring manner – 'Stand
up, be a Princess!' she would be told.

Up until then Carrie Fisher had only had one day's acting
work on a film set, seducing Warren Beatty in *Shampoo*. The
script's description of her character as 'beautiful' unnerved
her; she had been ordered to lose ten pounds but had only
managed half that: 'I didn't think I was pretty. I was a
Pilsbury doughgirl.'

Her part was always wooden. Princess Leia never quite
lives. But this is partly because of schisms in the character.
Her feminity is always under threat: she had a ram's-horn
hairdo; she was covered from neck to foot in a long white
gown; her breasts were held down with gaffer tape because,
she said facetiously, 'there was no sex in outer space'; we
first see her when she's firing her weapon.

Fisher had a British drama background and consequent accent. During the shooting of the film she was reading Colette 'just to be pretentious. I was very quiet. Whatever they asked me to do, I said, "Fantastic", because I didn't want to lose the job. I was also described as bovine and was told I'd inherited the worst qualities of both my parents.'

Arriving at Elstree from Tunisia, Lucas had ordered the sparkling sets created by John Barry, the production designer on *A Clockwork Orange*, to be dirtied up. A gleaming R2-D2 was rolled on the ground until it was scuffed and chipped. The director was similarly anxious that none of his cast should look other than lived-in and of their time: Luke's shirt was made from curtain-lining material, while Princess Leia's clothes looked as if they came from a Renaissance court.

And as George Lucas was Luke Skywalker, so Harrison Ford was Han Solo. The character had a deep background personal story: Solo had been raised by Wookies, expelled from the Space Academy, had a past as a spice smuggler and was an enemy of the Empire.

The pace of filming accelerated. By the final week's filming at Elstree, Lucas was operating three crews, one led by himself, another by Gary Kurtz, and a third by Robert Watts. In Los Angeles, meanwhile, where John Dykstra continued in his efforts to build a computer-controlled camera, Industrial Light and Magic had turned into a problem. ILM's two-storey warehouse in Van Nuys in the San Fernando Valley, the other side of the hills from Hollywood, was staffed largely by hippies: accordingly, it proceeded along a lateral, somewhat anarchic course that had the added fillip of generally being rather good fun for its employees. One hot summer's day, with the temperature soaring over the hundred-degree mark, the ILM employees rigged up an inflatable swimming-pool, running a chute to it from the building's roof. Just as the staff began plunging down into the water, a limousine's-worth of suitably startled Fox executives arrived.

Perhaps that kind of incident was a logical consequence of having the *Star Wars* special effects factory manned by young and relatively inexperienced people. Lucas had chosen young people not because of any abiding belief on his part in the creative zeal of youth, but so that he could have more control over them.

I wanted to be able to say, 'It must look like this, not that.' I don't want to be handed an effect at the end of five months and be told, 'Here's your special effect, sir.' I want to be able to have more say about what's going on . . . either you do it yourself, or you don't get a say.

Technically [Lucas told Stephen Zito] you always compare things against *2001*. If you took one of our shots and ran it on the light box and set it next to one of Kubrick's shots, you would say, 'Well, his are better.' But there is no way, given the time and money we've had, that Kubrick could do any better. He was striving for perfection and had a shot ratio thirty times what we have. When you spend that kind of time and money you can get things perfect. We went into this trying to make a cheap children's movie for $8 million. We didn't go in and say that we were going to make the perfect science fiction film, but we are gonna make the most spectacular thing you've ever seen!

All the same, there were communication problems between Dykstra and Lucas, as the special-effects expert explained to the same writer in 1997:

The major problem we encountered on this show was being able to apply what George started out with conceptually. From the day we met we talked about World War II dogfight footage which involved lots of action, continuous motion, moving camera, streak, loops and rolls, and all of the things aerial photography allows you to do in live action. This has been difficult to do in special effects with multiple ships, planet backgrounds and stars, because of the problem of angular displacement, matching shots and depth of field.

It's hard to explain that a concept won't work because of some technological thing, and this becomes a bone of contention. When a director shoots an exterior, he can see the lighting and the set-up and the action and hear the dialogue, but when he comes in here, all there is is a camera running down a track about three inches a second photographing a model . . .

The neat thing about George is that he has a sensibility. He is really involved in his movie, he is really attached. He's hard-headed about stuff, but, if he's wrong, he'll change his mind rather than say, 'I'm the director, I've made a decision and that's it.' He's got taste. He's got that gift for popular narrative. People like what he does: it's active; it's fast; there's humour in it. *Star Wars* is gonna be exciting all the way. The aerial battle that takes up the last reel of the film is going to be as exciting as the car chase in *The French Connection*.

But things were not always as amicable between them. When Lucas returned from England, ready to enter the cutting-room with his 340,000 feet of footage, he flew down to Los Angeles from San Francisco and went to see Dykstra. He could hardly believe what the ILM head honcho told him: that after a year's work ILM had spent a million dollars and come up with only three usable shots. Lucas lost it: furious, he screamed at Dykstra, who gave as good back.

During the flight back to San Francisco that evening, Lucas experienced severe chest pains. Hospitalized until the next day at Marin General Hospital, where he was diagnosed as suffering from extreme exhaustion, he spent a dark night of the soul in which he came to one overwhelming conclusion: that never again would he direct a film.

Making a motion picture on the scale of *Star Wars* carries continual potential for problems, especially those of a human kind. There were still some scenes Lucas needed to complete in California, notably the Mos Eisley Cantina sequence, which Lucas had intended as Dante's Inferno-in-Space. When Alan Ladd had to go to the Fox board to ask for an additional $20,000 to shoot the cantina scene, he played his ultimate card: *Star Wars*, he told the money-men, was the greatest picture ever made.

The cantina sequence, which is like a surreal vision of a classic western saloon-bar scene, was to be shot in the Californian desert; at the same time, Lucas would film the scenes featuring Luke's landspeeder in the Tatooine wilderness. On the morning of the shoot, however, Lucas learned that Mark Hamill had been in a serious car smash on the Pacific Coast Highway the previous evening: he was in Los Angeles County General Hospital with facial injuries. Accordingly a body double was employed and close-ups were avoided.

The ILM experience notwithstanding, science and technology generally could be more predictable than human frailty. Adversity had been turned to advantage through the need for blue-screening, which had turned out to be pure benediction. The final battle, in which the Death Star is destroyed, was based on a ten-minute montage of filmed aerial battles that Lucas assembled from such First and Second World War flying movies as *The Big Max*, *633 Squadron*, *Tora! Tora! Tora!*, *The Bridges of Toko-Ri* and *The Battle of Britain*. 'We cut them all together into a battle sequence to get an idea of the movement,' Gary Kurtz told *American Film*. 'It was a very bizarre-looking film – all black-and-white, a dirty 16mm dupe. There would be a shot of the pilot saying something, then you cut back to a long shot of the plane, explosions, crashes. It gave a reasonably accurate idea of what the battle sequence would look like, the feeling of it.'

These battle sequences were shown to special-effects experts and to artists who transferred this compilation to storyboards. 'It's very easy to take your hand and fly,' said Gary Kurtz. 'But it's very hard to convert that movement to what John Dykstra and the other special effects people had to do with the models.'

Perhaps most crucial of all was that the Star Destroyer at the beginning of the film should look credible: if the audience laughed, as they had been seen doing at R2-D2 during a Westwood cinema screening of forthcoming attractions, they were in trouble.

Where members of the production crew had simpler tasks, the results came more easily. Ben Burtt, for example, was a sound engineer extraordinaire.

Burtt's task, among others, was to seek out the exact sound that the *Millennium Falcon* and other craft would have. Accordingly, he went to Los Angeles International Airport, to military bases and to airshows recording the noise of screaming jet engines. The tone of the Imperial Cruisers engines, meanwhile, came from a slowing down of the sound of the advertising blimp used by Goodyear Tyres. He created the noise of the lasers by wacking a cable attached to a radio tower.

Burtt wasn't only a technohead. Intergalactic languages needed to be devised for the non-human characters. For Greedo, the bounty-hunting alien in the cantina, he came up with the idea of having him speak in Quechua, an extinct Incan language.

It was George Lucas who came to the conclusion that the voice of Dave Prowse, who played Darth Vader, was simply neither sufficiently evil nor aristocratic. What would be perfect would be the deep baritone of James Earl Jones, who had been nominated for an Academy Award for his lead role in *The Great White Hope*, the story of the first black boxer to become world champion. The fact that Jones was black was possibly not without intention: inadvertently, *Star Wars* had been cast without a single black actor.

George Lucas had applied to *Star Wars* the economies he had learned during the making of *American Graffiti*: fast-and-loose, hit-them-on-the-run film-making, but with a project that had taken a quantum leap in scope.

Towards the end of the production he admitted to Stephen Zito in *American Film* that many of his problems on the film had been a consequence of his chronic inability to delegate authority and responsibility:

I come up from the film-makers' school of doing movies, which means I do everything myself. If you are a writer-director, you must get involved with everything. It's very hard for me to get into another system where everybody does things for me, and I say, 'Fine.' If I ever continue to do these kinds of movies, I've got to learn to do that. I have a lot of friends who can, and I admire them. Francis Coppola is going through that now, and he's finally learning, finally getting to the point where he realizes he can't do it all. He's getting into the traditional system: 'Call me when it's ready and it better be right, and if it's not, do it again and spend whatever it costs to get it right.' But you have to be willing to make very expensive movies that way. You can't make cheap movies.

If I left anything for a day, it would fall apart, and it's purely because I set it up that way and there is nothing I can do about it. It wasn't set up so I could walk away from it. Whenever there is a leak in the dam, I have to stick my finger in it. I should learn to say, 'Somebody else go plug that up.'

For those film-makers who were close to him, George Lucas held a screening of a rough cut of *Star Wars* that had as yet had no music added: John Milius, Steven Spielberg, Matthew Robbins, Hal Barwood, Bill Huyck and Gloria Katz, Jay Cocks of *Time* magazine and Brian de Palma were all there.

None of them seemed colossally taken with the film – de Palma was especially disparaging, making jokes about the 'almighty Force' – except for Spielberg and Cocks who took him on one side and gave positive advice. Then de Palma redeemed himself by saying that he and Jay Cocks would rewrite the opening crawl that gave the story's background.

But the film took a quantum leap when John Williams' music was added soon after. Williams' soundtrack took the classic form of an expanded cliff-hanger serial, brimming with dramatic counterpoints and changes: the composer based much of this work on the musical influence of Erich Korngold, who had scored such great Errol Flynn swash-bucklers as *Robin Hood*, *The Sea Hawk* and *Captain Blood*. In some scenes the excitement, which seemed to stem from the magic of special effects, was simply an emotional response to the power of Williams' epic score. His music immeasurably expanded the movie, swamping nearly every frame and commenting alertly on the action. Lucas thought that working with John Williams was 'wonderful: just the way life should be.'

'It's the underpinning, a grease that each movie slides along on and a glue that holds it together so that you can follow it,' Lucas told Paul Scanlon in *Rolling Stone* in 1983. 'There's always been a scene or a moment in which the music connects so strongly with the visual that it sends shivers up my spine every time I see it.'

Deals had been struck with Marvel comics and Del Rey books – although initially the toy industry was harder to bust through. Lucas' experience on *THX 1138*, however, had shown him precisely who was his base market – science fiction fans.

And so this was who was targeted: such visible aspects of the Star Wars Corporation as Ralph McQuarrie's sketches and assorted story-boards were taken on a tour of science fiction conventions across the United States throughout the winter before the film was due to open; at the World Science Fiction Convention in Kansas City not only was there a sparkling C-3PO and a full-size model of Darth Vader, but Mark 'Luke Skywalker' Hamill was there to enlighten onlookers about the models of the *Millennium Falcon*, droids and other hardware.

When his film opened, George Lucas wanted to make sure that at least some people would come to it. After all, gloomy prognostications continued to dribble forth from Fox: now the studio's research was arguing that the word 'war' in a title was a no-no – women simply would not go to see such a film, insisted the marketing men. At first the film seemed a hard sell: after the negative responses to the preview trailers, they were pulled from cinemas. At the urging of Lucas to Ladd, *Star Wars* was pitched through teenage media, even through advertisements on cable television in college dormitories.

The studio, in fact, believed that its only sure-fire hit for 1977 would be *The Other Side of Midnight*: a Second World War story – subject-matter that its bland, catch-all title steered safely away from – by Sidney Sheldon, starring Marie-France Pisier, John Beck and Susan Sarandon. Fox even gave some cinema owners a choice: book *Star Wars*, or they would not get *The Other Side of Midnight*. Later the studio was fined $25,000 for this.

To be economically viable, *Star Wars* needed to be under two hours long. When final cutting-room sacrifices were

required, Lucas completely removed all scenes and refer-
ences to Biggs Darklighter (played by Garrick Hagon),
Luke's fellow rebel pilot and boyhood friend. Not wanting
the film to be saddled with the slur of 'kid's-movie', Lucas
and Kurtz pushed for a 'PG' rating – and got it.

On 25 May 1977, *Star Wars* opened in the United States in
thirty-two cinemas. In New York and Los Angeles shows
began at 10 a.m. In each case there were long queues two
hours before.

Some were drawn by science fiction freaks' word-of-
mouth. Most came, however, because the picture had drawn
superlative reviews. 'I loved *Star Wars*,' wrote Jack Kroll in
Newsweek, 'and so will you . . .' And in the rival *Time* Lucas
got six pages of coverage, with the banner headline '*Star
Wars*: The Year's Best Movie', and adulation in the prose that
described it as 'a grand and glorious film that may well be
the smash hit of 1977 . . . a subliminal history of movies,
wrapped in a riveting tale of suspense and adventure, orna-
mented with some of the most ingenious special effects ever
contrived for film.' In *Variety*, meanwhile, Harrison Ford was
selected as 'outstanding'.

By titling it *Star Wars IV: A New Hope*, the makers of the film
established a sense that everything we were about to see we
somehow were already familiar with: which we were, of course,
as Lucas had dredged most of its characters and themes from
the collective unconscious of mythology.

Star Wars stomped all over the other contenders – *The
Deep*, *Sorcerer*, *Exorcist: The Heretic* – in that summer of
1977; *Smokey and the Bandit* was the only other substantial
box-office success. More than one in twenty filmgoers in

1977 saw *Star Wars* more than once. When the film was released, Fox's stock was $12 a share. Four years later it went for $70 a share.

From now on, the movie business was to be changed for ever.

For the Academy Awards to be held in April of the next year, *Star Wars* received ten nominations: these included Best Direction, Best Screenplay and Best Picture. Along with Richard Chew and Paul Hirsch, Marcia Lucas was nominated for the Best Editing award. Other contenders were John Barry for art direction, John Mollo for costume design, John Williams for musical score, and John Dykstra, Richard Edlund, Grant McCune, John Stears, and Robert Blalack for special effects.

The special-effects team, who had literally sent Lucas sick to hospital, won their nomination, as did sound man Ben Burtt. But the only award the Lucas family received went to Marcia for her editing, along with Chew and Hirsch: as he had been with *American Graffiti*, George Lucas was kept completely out of the awards loop, overshadowed by Woody Allen's more 'sophisticated' *Annie Hall*, which took the awards for Best Picture, Best Direction and Best Screenplay. Whether it was because of the slickness with which he tied up Hollywood in deals that suited him, rather than vice versa, or simply because of jealousy at a colossal success that seemed to come out of left-field, George Lucas - like his friend Steven Spielberg at the time — never won a major Academy Award. Clearly, he was to be kept soundly in his place.

Buoyed by the Oscar night publicity, Fox re-released the film that summer: it quickly took in another $46 million in tickets. It was not until November 1978 that *Star Wars* finally ended its run in US cinemas: by then it was the number one grossing film of all time, having taken $273 million gross. With overseas markets added on, *Star Wars* grossed $430 million by the end of 1979, and for the first time Hollywood studios had come to understand the significance of foreign sales.

5 Sand, Plans and More Graffiti

How did George Lucas survive *Star Wars*-mania? By the surest known method of not being overcome by one's success: he simply didn't take it very seriously.

As soon as the film was released, George and Marcia Lucas went on holiday, to Maui, their first vacation since 1969. Soon Lucas was joined there by Steven Spielberg. Mythic reverberations, cod 'inner child' psychology and comic absurdity: each jockeyed for position as Lucas celebrated the success of *Star Wars* by constructing a sand-castle with his fellow director. As they played on the beach, the two men opened up about their filmic dreams.

What did Spielberg tell Lucas he wanted to do? To make a picture like a James Bond film. Why not, asked Lucas, drawing on a favoured source of inspiration, structure it in the style of the Thirties and Forties movie serials? What's more, he said, he already had had some thoughts along these lines. 'I said, "I've got a great idea. And I can't get anybody interested in it." So I told him the idea, and he said, "That's fantastic! I'd love to do that." And that's really how it got started.'

Lucas outlined to Spielberg an idea he had come up with a couple of years previously about a playboy adventurer: in

1975 he and film-maker Phil Kaufman had spent three weeks dreaming up a film idea about such a character that was based on Adolf Hitler's obsession with acquiring ancient religious artefacts, specifically, the Ark of the Covenant – a notion given full flight in the then popular book *Spear of Destiny*. Spielberg loved the idea and they agreed to make the film.

'*Raiders* was an old project that I had even before *Star Wars*, and I was trying to get people to do it. At one point Phil Kaufman was having a difficult time with his career,' Lucas told *Film Comment*, 'so I said, "I've got this great movie. C'mon, let's do this picture, and we'll get Francis, or somebody, to get us a deal somewhere." So I told him the story, and he told me about the ark and all that stuff, and we had about half a dozen story conferences over the period of about three weeks . . .' At the end of that period, however, Kaufman was offered the job of directing *The Outlaw Josey Wales* – he was subsequently fired from the film, its star Clint Eastwood taking over the director's chair.

With the project revived, Lucas and Spielberg agreed to work on it, and to seek out a writer. For now, however, there was further work on the schedule.

Star Wars had made George Lucas $20 million wealthier. But he put all this money into safe investments: he would be needing it soon, he knew, as he intended to finance the sequel to *Star Wars* himself. In the end the director – or producer, as he was now to be – lent this $20 million to Lucasfilm as collateral to finance *The Empire Strikes Back*, as *Star Wars 2* came to be called. The only addition to the lifestyle of George Lucas seemed to be the used Ferrari the former cruiser now drove around in. By this time, the cash was coming in from the assorted *Star Wars* merchandising deals: Lucasfilm would shortly be ringing up around $10 million a year from toys alone.

Others around him who had been in the film benefited fabulously. With his 0.25 per cent of the net, Harrison Ford did not do badly. Yet he was nowhere near the financial league of the far more experienced Sir Alec Guinness, whose deal gave him 2.5 per cent of gross royalties – he earned more from playing Obi-Wan Kenobi than from all his other film roles put together. On a creative level, moreover, Guinness considered Lucas to be the apotheosis of directors, and delivered the ultimate compliment: George Lucas, said Sir Alec, had a similar 'eye' to Sir David Lean.

More American Graffiti

Before he was free to move on to his next space adventure, George Lucas was committed to completing a sequel to *American Graffiti* for Universal. To make the first film he had agreed to a three-picture deal – the third film, *Radioland Murders*, would not appear until 1994.

In 1971 Lucas had been taken with an impressive film called *Cisco Pike*, a Los Angeles-set counter-culture story about the world of drug-dealing which starred Gene Hackman and Kris Kristofferson. *Cisco Pike* developed a cult reputation that has stood the test of time. Yet its subject-matter had proved a poisoned chalice for Bill Norton, its young writer-director, another USC alumnus whom Lucas had known when he was studying there. As had been the experience of the Zoetrope partners, the kind of 'alternative' cinema that once would have got you on to the cover of

Rolling Stone no longer impressed Hollywood moguls; Norton had not directed any more movies. Subsequently he had made his living by script-writing, which seemed a good enough reason for George Lucas to contact him: 'He said that if he liked the script, I could direct it.'

Norton discovered that Lucas already had the four main stories of the film, to be called *More American Graffiti*, which was set on four New Year's Eves from 1964 to 1967. The gang from the first film have finished high school two years previously. Paul Le Mat is still racing cars; Cindy Williams is pregnant with Ron Howard's child; Wolfman Jack is back, hectoring the USA with his street wisdom, spinning songs from the mid-Sixties.

What Lucas decided was that he personally would executive produce *More American Graffiti*, and that his former USC classmate Howard Kazanjian would be the actual producer. Bill Norton, as he had hoped, was given the directing job.

The multiple stories, however, proved a problem and the film did not seem to hang together. 'In *More American Graffiti* we were asking a lot of the audience, because things were happening at different times, as well as in different places,' said Norton.

The job of editor was given to Tina Hirsch, a relative of *Star Wars* editor Paul Hirsch. But Lucas took over as soon as she handed in her first cut. This became his practice: he would let a hired director deliver his first cut, but step in personally if he felt it necessary.

In Lucas's canon of work, *More American Graffiti* is something of a footnote: it only broke even two years after its 1979 release, following sales to pay television.

6 The Empire Strikes Back

After such a success as *Star Wars*, only the best would do for its sequel. To write the film George Lucas accordingly hired Leigh Brackett, the author of science-fiction novels and the co-writer of such cinema classics as *The Big Sleep* and *Rio Bravo*. Lucas admired the terseness of the speech, the straight narrative drive of her films. In March 1978 she handed in her first draft: for Lucas her hard-boiled dialogue was just what he needed – the script was going in the direction he wanted. But two weeks later Leigh Brackett died of cancer.

It seemed like a curious twist of fate. For the third time in a row this man who loathed writing – yet had proved colossally successful when doing it – was obliged to write the script himself: there is something funny and endearing about the image of this magician-like figure tucked away in his room, extracting the essence of a film drop by drop.

Right through the summer of 1978 he laboured, all the while looking for a writer to take over from him. Then he realized this figure was right in front of him. Steven Spielberg had held Lucas to his sandy handshake and gone ahead with *Raiders of the Lost Ark*, as their 1930s playboy-adventurer movie had come to be titled. At Spielberg's suggestion,

Lawrence Kasdan had been hired to write the film; Kasdan was a former advertising copywriter who had written *Continental Divide*, a comedy that Spielberg had almost directed. When Kasdan flew up to San Francisco to deliver the first *Raiders of the Lost Ark* draft, Lucas asked him to take over the *Empire* writing job before he'd even looked at it. 'I said, "Don't you want to read this first?" George said, "Well, if I hate it tonight, I'll call you up and take back the offer. But I just get a feeling about people." '

With a writer finally on board, Lucas made his announcement that he personally would finance *The Empire Strikes Back*. And Fox would distribute it.

The Empire Strikes Back had three acts, each around thirty-five minutes long. Just as Lucas had wanted, the structure of the 105-page screenplay that Lawrence Kasdan turned in was a precise reflection of this. Lucas had told him that he needed to establish rapidly who were the main characters and then quickly set these up in the first experiences they were to undergo. For the sake of visual continuity, Lucas once again employed Norman Reynolds as production designer and Ralph McQuarrie as illustrator.

So that audiences could see this was a new film, however, Lucas made sure that new creatures and settings were introduced at the beginning of the movie. And an important new plot possibility was brought out as early as possible: Lucas wanted to implant in the minds of the audience the idea that Luke might kill Vader, with all its implications of patricide.

The basic plot, as sketched out by Lucas first to Leigh Brackett and then to Lawrence Kasdan was revenge drama of the almost classically Elizabethan formula: Luke tries to save his friends from Darth Vader; Vader in turn uses Han, Princess Leia and Chewbacca as his bait to trap Luke, whom he is trying to switch to the dark side of the Force. Key elements from *Star Wars* were reintroduced almost immediately: the rebellion against the Empire; the love/hate relationship between Princess Leia and Han Solo; the rivalry/loyalty between Han and Luke; the platonic affection between Luke and Leia.

And the notion of the Force was expanded even further. Obi-Wan Kenobi, killed by Vader in the previous film, was now only a shadowy apparition. For the first time the Emperor was given a physical presence – a hooded figure with an aura of infinite evil of whom even Darth Vader was scared.

As a counter-balance, the character of Yoda was introduced. Twenty-six inches tall, Yoda was the guru-like Jedi master and sage, an 800-year-old shaman. The model of Yoda was worked on for over a year: Stuart Freeborn, the designer, based Yoda's image on a picture of Albert Einstein set against his own reflection. Yoda's voice and operating were performed by Frank Oz, the Muppet master who had fulfilled the same functions for Miss Piggy.

In the scene on Dagobah, the bog planet, in which Yoda attempts to initiate Luke Skywalker into the way of the Jedi warrior, many of the essential precepts are those of Buddhism. (To create the visual realism, an Elstree sound stage was filled with ankle-deep water, which was then sprayed with mineral oils.)

There were other new locations: the ice planet Hoth, which was the rebels' army base until they were attacked by imperial troops. And Bespin's Cloud City, ostensibly reigned over by Han Solo's old friend, the new character of Lando

Calrissian, played by Billy Dee Williams, a black actor who had first come to Lucas's attention when he saw him playing opposite Diana Ross in the Billie Holiday biopic, *Lady Sings the Blues*: given the subliminal history of how James Earl Jones came to be hired for the voice of Darth Vader, you might feel that here a certain amount of political correctness was being exercised.

Although both Lawrence Kasdan and Gary Kurtz had been concerned that the script suffered from a lack of scene-by-scene emotional resolution, Lucas's response was simple: give 'em enough action, and no one will notice. He wasn't being glib here: simply covering up his recurrent fear of delivering work that was too slow. 'The trick is to know what you can leave to the audience's imagination,' Lucas told Dale Pollock, his official biographer. 'If they start getting lost, you're in trouble. Sometimes you have to be crude and just say what's going on, because if you don't, people get puzzled.' Besides, the action-enhancing special effects in *The Empire Strikes Back* – as in both the other *Star Wars* films – were always driven by the story and never existed simply for their own ends.

Wanting to expand his career, Harrison Ford had been reluctant to return to the part of Han Solo. He would only do so, he said, if the script showed his Solo character undergoing considerable development. What he especially felt was needed was a real love triangle between himself, Luke and Leia. As this was precisely what had been developed in the screenplay, he agreed to climb aboard the project.

Who would direct the film? Gary Kurtz again was to be the film's line producer. And he knew a man who seemed perfect for the job. He had first met Irvin Kershner, another former USC graduate who had also taught on the film course, while he was directing *Stakeout on Dope Street*, an anti-drugs documentary, back in 1958. More recently he had made *The Eyes of Laura Mars*, a thriller with a troubled production history originally written by John Carpenter; more crucially for Lucas, in 1976 Kershner had directed *The Return of a Man Called Horse*, a sequel that eclipsed the original in almost every way.

Now in his late forties, Kershner was a man of many parts; he was also, for example, a classical musician. And he had a reputation for working fast. A vegetarian and Buddhist (the character of Yoda was to appeal to him), Kershner was very taken with the notion of the Force: having assiduously researched fairy-tales and mythology himself, he had seen how effectively one could thereby reach the subconscious of audiences.

Even though he was also a student of Zen, Kershner was worried about the danger of losing control through working with Lucas. He was, however, hardly likely to turn down an opportunity to join the dream team that had made *Star Wars*. So, in order to circumvent potential problems, Kershner sketched out every shot in the film: eventually he had a book of drawings nine inches thick. He made two copies of this, and gave one to Lucas; then he departed to the winter of Norway, where the scenes on the ice planet Hoth were to be filmed before sound-stage work commenced, again at Elstree. Irvin Kershner proved the opposite of Lucas when it came to handling actors: he was more than open to improvisation and debate. The director and Harrison Ford empathized well.

In the first week in March 1979, almost one hundred foreigners descended on the tiny Norwegian hamlet of Finse, more than doubling its population. The hinterland of Finse had been chosen as the location for the surface of the ice planet Hoth. Finse had been the training camp for Captain Scott before he set out on his fatal expedition to the South Pole. So it seemed hardly inappropriate that, as soon as all the equipment was in place in Norway and Carrie Fisher and Mark Hamill had installed themselves in the Finse ski lodge, a furious snow blizzard raged and avalanches cut them off from the rest of the world.

The winter of 1978–9 was the worst in Europe for many years. So filming on *The Empire Strikes Back*, which began on 5 March, was following the familiar pattern of the beginning of shoots on George Lucas movies. This dreadful, dangerous weather forced Plan B to be enacted. Shooting was re-scheduled and Harrison Ford flew in from London, only just managing to make it through the blizzards to the location. Kershner had opted to shoot the scene in which Han prevents Luke from freezing to death by wrapping him in his dead Tauntaun – he is saved by the last remaining body heat from this fantastical beast, a creature devised by Lucas as appropriate for the emerging mythology of a new time.

The weather conditions were the coldest in which anyone involved with the film had ever worked. Harrison and Hamill both wore two pairs of thermal pants and four pairs of socks. The camera equipment had to have lightweight oil put into it to prevent it from freezing up. If you touched a camera without wearing gloves your skin would freeze to the metal: the only way to free yourself was by slicing it away with a razor blade. In this extreme cold the film would become brittle and crack.

For seven weeks they worked in conditions in which ten degrees below zero was considered warm. For days at a time the crew would be snowed into their motel. By the time they headed for England, only 33,000 of the required 75,000 feet of film had been shot.

At least it had been warm at Elstree: on 24 January, much of the studio had gone up in flames. Stanley Kubrick, who was there making *The Shining*, had been delayed in his filming and was unable to vacate the sound stages he was using. In his turn Kubrick now slowed down Gary Kurtz in his set building, which had to be ready for when the crew arrived from Norway at the end of April.

Once filming began at Elstree there were further problems, exemplified by the fact that many of the electronic gadgets simply didn't work. Although the involvement of Muppet co-creator Frank Oz had filled senior members of the team with great confidence, no one knew if Yoda was actually going to respond in the manner in which it was intended.

As director of photography, Peter Schuzitsky, who had shot the Ken Russell extravaganza *Lisztomania*, replaced Gil Taylor, the *Star Wars* cinematographer. But *Empire* was not without its measure of tragedy: on 6 June art director John Barry collapsed, complaining of a headache. He died within hours in hospital, of infectious meningitis.

The involvement of Sir Alec Guinness had also initially been in jeopardy: eight months before production began he had developed a serious, sight-threatening eye infection. Luckily, he recovered.

Over two years had passed since Mark Hamill's car crash. Despite having undergone plastic surgery, he still bore some facial scars from the accident: seeing this, George Lucas wrote in a scene in which Luke had been mauled by a Wampa, then healed.

What was the hardest thing to do in the shooting of *Empire*? To freeze Han Solo in the large block of carbonite that ends the film. Irvin Kershner's concept was that this sequence would resemble a mad-scientist film of the 1930s: central to it would be a forty-foot cylinder of spiralling metals and gushing steam, melting plastic objects and emitting fumes; the sequence had a German Expressionist graphic quality, especially the Shroud-like woodcut of Han Solo in carbon freeze.

It was apparent that this was a more physically exacting film than *Star Wars*. 'This one would have laid George out,' said Gary Kurtz. All the same, although Irvin Kershner directed it, people still think of *The Empire Strikes Back* as a George Lucas film and are largely unaware that another director was at the helm. As had been the case with Bill Norton and *More American Graffiti*, Lucas gave Kershner his first cut . . . and then re-edited the film himself with Marcia.

Although the original budget for *The Empire Strikes Back* had been $15 million, it had gone up to $18.5 million, almost twice the cost of *Star Wars*, before shooting even began. In the intervening three years, the cost of making films had risen dramatically. This was partly because *Star Wars* had established a new set of ground rules: in *The Empire Strikes Back*, there were over 600 'opticals', or special effects shots – twice the number used in *Star Wars*.

Once production started, making the film was costing Lucas nearly $100,000 a day. And he was almost excessively conscious that it was his own money that was being spent, often referring to this. Moreoever, this was a time when the value of the pound against the dollar suddenly soared: when *Star Wars* had been made, one English pound would buy around 1.55 dollars; just before shooting began on *Empire*, after all costs had been locked in place, the pound soared to around the 2.40 dollar mark, a huge difference when it came to paying costs and wages in the UK.

A few weeks into filming, Gary Kurtz had to tell Lucas that the film would cost $22 million. Although Lucas had been given his first production loan from the established movie money supply line, the Bank of America in Los Angeles, it refused to give him the extra $6 million he suddenly found he needed.

In the end Lucas had to go with his hat out to Fox to ask the studio to guarantee a loan of $3 million from First National Bank of Boston. Fox agreed – in exchange for fifteen per cent of the *Empire* profits. Currency fluctuations notwithstanding, Lucas was deeply unhappy that the team of Kurtz and Kershner eventually went $10 million over budget. After all, always hanging over him was the grim spectre of Francis Coppola's huge financial overage on *Apocalypse Now*.

The Empire Strikes Back was scheduled for release by Twentieth Century Fox on 21 May 1980. The studio, however, was not happy: its feeling was that the deal Lucas had struck for himself was so advantageous that it would become the laughing-stock of Hollywood. Yet Fox had begun to be somewhat mollified by the $26 million it took from cinema owners in advance bookings.

Fans began lining up outside the Egyptian Theater in Hollywood three days before the film opened. After six days the box office was through the $9 million mark. Three months on from 21 May, Lucas had his investment back. *Empire* easily eclipsed its nearest box-office rival that summer, the counter-culture extravaganza *The Blues Brothers*, starring John Belushi and Dan Ackroyd. (That summer's other hits? *Fame*, *Brubaker*, *Rough Cut*, *Can't Stop the Music*.) *The Empire Strikes Back* sold more than 300 million tickets around the world. And Fox earned $40 million in distribution fees. At the beginning of the 1990s it was the third most successful film of all time, behind *E.T.* and *Star Wars*.

As a result, perhaps, of the same small thinking that had Fox worried they would be laughed at in Hollywood, and that was possibly also responsible for Lucas never receiving a major Academy Award, he then ran into an egregious piece of pettiness on the part of the Directors Guild of America.

In accordance with the film's visual style, Irvin Kershner's credit was not shown at the beginning of the film: the template had been set on *Star Wars*, where the opening crawl of text gave the story's background, and Lucas had not credited himself until the end of the film. Because of this, Lucas received a communication from the Directors Guild of America, fining him $250,000. Finally, Lucas settled out of court for $25,000 after having been threatened by the DGA that all copies of the film would have to be removed from cinemas if the issue went to arbitration.

7 Raiders of the Lost Ark

Before plunging into the hell of writing *The Empire Strikes Back*, George Lucas had met Steven Spielberg and Lawrence Kasdan in Los Angeles for a brainstorming session on *Raiders of the Lost Ark*. The location was Lucas's small office on Lankershim Boulevard in north Hollywood, across the way from Universal.

Spielberg was somewhat bemused by Lucas's suggestion that the lead character be named Indiana: he was only too aware that this was the name of George Lucas's dog. All the same, they seemed to be a potentially strong team: Spielberg shoots on the hoof, filming the action as it enfolds; for his part, Lucas can already see what this will look like in the cutting-room; Kasdan's writing, moreover, had an immediacy and wit that heightened its powerful narrative drive.

'Larry Kasdan, Steve and I worked together on it, but basically when I laid out the story, it was fairly articulate,' Lucas told *Film Comment*. 'Every scene was described. They changed and personalized it a lot the way they wanted, but essentially the concept remained the same.'

Spielberg wanted *Raiders* to be like a Disneyland ride; Lucas wanted it to be true to the serials of the 1930s.

Together they watched fifteen episodes of *Don Winslow of the Navy* . . . and came to the conclusion that it was actually not very good at all, in writing, acting or direction – it simply didn't stand the test of time.

The cinema matinee serials, they realized, could be no more than a starting-point: they needed to create something entirely original. Lucas sketched out his vision: *Raiders of the Lost Ark*, as the film was to be called, was to be a seven-act film divided into sixty scenes, each two pages long. There would be six cliff-hanger moments – every twenty pages there would be a new piece of excitement. 'The advantage that *Raiders* had was that there was no previous film. He was sort of establishing certain criteria that wouldn't be in conflict with anything else. When I wrote *Raiders*, I actually wrote four stories, four different stories. One of them was a very action-oriented kind of thing, which was what Steve wanted to do. I would watch that he didn't go against what the character was supposed to be throughout the series. The character has to be consistent. Some of his traits Steve wasn't enamoured with and wanted to avoid.'

The model for Indiana Jones was to be Humphrey Bogart in *Treasure of the Sierra Madre*. Although he would be an unscrupulous academic playboy, who financed his work by selling dubiously obtained antiquities, he was still a highly moral figure, with a developed sense of right and wrong, insisted Lucas: 'Steve wanted to make him a lot sleazier at home. He was for a while very anxious to have him be an alcoholic, and I said no.'

They came to an impasse. Then Spielberg suggested the Jones character was 'just like Harrison Ford'. Lucas was completely against hiring anyone who wasn't a new film face:

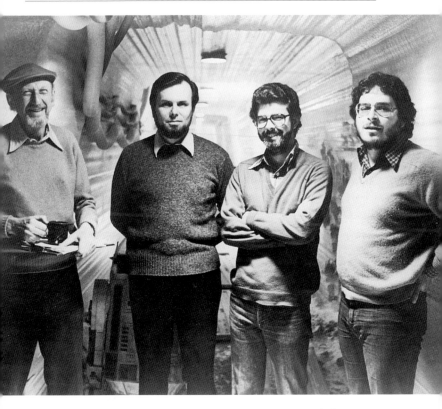

On the set of The Empire Strikes Back. **From left: director Irvin Kershner, producer Gary Kurtz, executive producer George Lucas and screenwriter Lawrence Kasdan.**

he had already been trying to get Tom Selleck for the part, but had found he couldn't get him out of the contract he had for *Magnum, P.I.* – Selleck had only made a pilot for the programme, but as soon as CBS learned of this high level interest in him, they put the series into their upcoming schedule.

Spielberg eventually talked Lucas into using Ford: there was a phrase he loved to use about the actor that he felt summed up the man and why he fitted the part so perfectly – 'grizzled irrepressibility'. Finally, Lucas went for the idea. (Ford, however, did not immediately understand why he had been especially selected for the role: 'George, the man's a grave-robber!' he told Lucas.)

'Indiana Jones is a college professor – on the one hand, a professor of archaeology, anthropology, and on the other hand, he's sort of a soldier of fortune,' Lucas told *Film Comment* shortly before the picture was released.

He's a sleazy kind of character, who is right on the edge of legality in terms of the ways he acquires things and deals a great deal with the occult. He's really an expert on the occult. Those are the two sides of him that are shown in *Raiders*. They're essential to the story. But Indiana is also a 1930s playboy. He has nights on the town and spends a lot of money.

He doesn't get that from teaching college. The original irony was: here's this college professor. How can he get enough money to live this other life that he's living with all these girls and these fancy cars and furs and stuff? Well, the secret of it is – how he acquires it – is by buying antiquities, which he sells for a great deal of money to museums, and that's to finance his habit.

At this LA story conference, Lucas talked Spielberg and Kasdan out of their big ideas. The logic was always crucial: would the audience be able to follow it? 'Films grow complicated and film-makers forget why they're making them,' he kept insisting to them.

Indiana Jones, it was established, would have two enemies: a rival French archaeologist and a slimy Nazi. Marion Ravenwood, the heroine, to be played by Karen Allen (Debra Winger had been first choice, but was unavailable), was not far removed from Princess Leia in spirit: self-assured, arrogant, and capable of pulling the trigger one last time. It was Marcia Lucas, however, who spotted that because Marion disappears from the plot there was no emotional resolution to the film: this was accordingly corrected.

Apart from that glitch, the plot was exceedingly strong, again dealing in the same archetypal areas that Lucas had so effectively mined in *Star Wars*. It was clear who were the good and who were the bad guys: and in Christian-Judaic culture there could hardly be a more profoundly resonant quest than the archaeologist adventurer's search for the Ark of the Covenant.

The creative package had been put together. Now a financial deal had to be struck. Hardly a problem, surely? These two men had, after all, made *American Graffiti*, *Star Wars*, *Jaws*, and *Close Encounters of the Third Kind*, the most successful films of all time.

'Let's make a creative deal. Let's go for a deal that will make history,' George Lucas urged Spielberg. The result was that every studio except one turned them down. The deal they were trying to strike was virtually prohibitive. The studio would put down the $20 million needed to make the film – originally it had been costed at $7 million, and it ended up as $22 million. After the money was recouped, it would be split sixty-forty between Lucas and the studio. After rentals had reached $50 million, the split would be fifty-fifty. After $100 million it would be forty-sixty.

Only Michael Eisner at Paramount, spurred on by his second-in-command Jeffrey Katzenberg, was prepared to go for Lucas's 'killer deal'. In the end the studio made $49 million in rentals from *Raiders*; Spielberg personally made $22 million; and Lucasfilm made $21. Its success allowed Paramount to make a dozen other films.

Having put the movie into motion, Lucas worked on *Raiders* until it started shooting. He also kept a sharp eye on the budget, reducing some of Spielberg's more extravagant requirements: two thousand extras were cut to just six hundred; a four-engined flying boat became a two-engined flying boat.

Deciding that he would see the initial shooting was running smoothly, George Lucas went to Tunisia. But on the very first day he was so badly sunburned that his skin was permanently damaged: his face now turns bright red if exposed to the sun.

Apart from that personal tragedy, filming went smoothly: Lucas had wanted *Raiders* shot in eighty-five days – speedy Spielberg had the job done in seventy-three. Perhaps in the hands of even the hammiest of directors, its subject-matter alone – essentially, *The Quest for the Holy Grail* – could have helped to give *Raiders of the Lost Ark* its high philosophical dimensions. But at his finest, as in *Schindler's*

List, the great populist that is Steven Spielberg can connect with the purest essence of a theme. In *Raiders* every intellectual muscle and intuitive brain cell are at peak tone, honed to perfection by his working partnership with George Lucas. Simple effects are used for simple ideas so effectively that by the end of the film, your belief is utterly suspended and you are carried breathtakingly away by the profundity of the sight of the melting villains choking on their own precious bodily fluids.

'When it was finished, I took over the editing. Spielberg did a first cut, and said, "This is as good as I can make it." I had the film for about a month after that, and I recut it,' said Lucas. All the same, he considered *Raiders of the Lost Ark* ('I think it will be a hit,' he suggested modestly to *Film Comment*) to be a Steven Spielberg film when it is just as much a George Lucas one.

There was an irony here. While Spielberg had hoped to found a Disney-like empire, Lucas had wanted to make his career as a director. But after *Raiders* he described Spielberg as 'the most naturally talented director I've ever met. Whatever talent I have is . . . being in tune with mass sensibility. My talent is not particularly in making films.' In turn, Spielberg described Lucas thus: 'If he wasn't a movie-maker, he'd run a newspaper; he'd be Charles Foster Kane.'

With the success of *The Empire Strikes Back* and *Raiders of the Lost Ark*, which was released in 1981, George Lucas had become the most successful film-maker in the history of motion pictures. The fact that Spielberg's *E.T.*, released the next year, replaced *Star Wars* as the biggest box-office success of all time did little to tarnish this glory.

Furthermore, the gamble of personally financing *The Empire Strikes Back* had paid off. Although it had come close to bankrupting him, it had made George Lucas rich beyond his dreams. And now he started using this money for the purpose for which it had been intended all along.

In Marin County, some thirty miles north of San Francisco's Golden Gate Bridge, George Lucas chose and bought five thousand acres of land. Here, at the end of a mile-long narrow valley with its own creek, he would build Skywalker Ranch, intending it to be his base of operations.

The word 'ranch', with its frontier connotations, was something of a romantic, film world misnomer: it was really a re-created Victorian hamlet of vaguely New England-style cottages and sheds around a multi-turreted mansion. This main house was furnished with extraordinary opulence: expensive antiques, Victorian trimmings, lamps and stained glass were all chosen by Marcia Lucas. With carefully rusted antique farm machinery in its pastures, the premises also had their own old red-brick winery. The winery was built in 1870, Lucas would claim, and the cottages later. Here, however, he was simply creating an elaborate back story for the property, as befitted a man who had contrived an entire new mythology for *Star Wars*: the truth was that, like a Disney frontier ride, the place had been built from scratch. (Not that Lucas always noticed his surroundings or even other individuals: like many creative people, living deep inside his thoughts, he would pass people in corridors and hardly seem to see them.)

On Skywalker Ranch, in fact, there are fourteen fantasy structures concealing a secret movie factory with all the most up-to-date, computerized film-editing and sound equipment that modern film-making has to offer: there is a sound stage, for example, big enough to hold the Los Angeles Philharmonic orchestra. Down the valley are administrative offices, sufficient for 450 staff, an archive building, a games complex with pools, stables, tennis courts, gyms and a child-care room. The creek spills over man-made waterfalls into an artificial lake. In the end, George Lucas was to spend over $60 million on building a property that might be considered to rival Citizen Kane's *Xanadu*.

'I love it,' the producer-director explained to Audie Bock of *Take One* magazine as they sat in the heat of the new Lucasfilm offices in the rambling Victorian house that houses them. 'It reminds me of the Central Valley around Modesto where I grew up – hot, dry heat and nothing but walnut groves. I thrive on it. In fact when we first came to this area to set up American Zoetrope, I wanted to settle in Marin. Francis is more of a city person, so we ended up in San Francisco, but now I'm doing what I always wanted to do.'

Like one of those children who have been brought up by a father who is terrible with money, Lucas had vowed that he would never follow the heartstoppingly catastrophic financial example of Francis Ford Coppola, his mentor. In addition, Lucas had not forgotten that *THX 1138* and *American Graffiti* were taken away from him, and that Fox dogged his heels throughout the making of *Star Wars*. He simply did not trust Hollywood, and wanted to be far from it. Fair and amicable with everyone until wronged, Lucas then would never forgive or forget: sometimes he seemed to think his ability to hold a grudge was some kind of virtue.

Among the many ambitious facilities at his new headquarters, such as state-of-the-art film projection equipment, was its library: this contains sounds and clips catalogued according to subject. And the genesis of Skywalker Ranch, Lucas told Bock, went back as far as his first film.

> I cut *THX* in the attic of that house in Mill Valley. One downstairs bedroom had been turned into a sound studio. I would cut during the day and Walter Murch would come in and cut sound effects during the night. Then, when I started to do *Graffiti*, I finally convinced Francis that what he really needed was to buy a house out here we could work at, because I wasn't going to work in the city. So we bought a house, and I cut *Graffiti* there in an apartment over the garage.
>
> After *Graffiti* became a hit, I bought my own big Victorian house, built a screening room in the back, and used it for my base of operations. I made *Star Wars* there and *More American Graffiti*.
>
> Then I decided I would build a new version of it out at the house. Essentially all the ranch is is a big Victorian house that's used as offices. It's got a library and it's got a screening room. It's for writers and for post-production, and eventually the sound-mixing facility will be moved out there.

Anxious to build permanent financial security that didn't depend on the whims of cinema, Lucas had made a decision to use merchandising as a financial foundation from which to diversify into areas separate from film. And he put together a $5 million computer company to pursue the possibilities of what would become digital editing. Taken with video games ever since he had first encountered an onscreen ping-pong tournament, Lucas — years before most other people were alerted to such an idea — was also interested in the possibil-

ities of more sophisticated electronic developments such as
multi-media.

But what was all this colossal expense and ingenuity really
about? It was so that Lucas's film headquarters at Skywalker
Ranch should recreate the atmosphere of his film school
days and the consequent creative hothouse of USC: 'Room
108, where we had screenings going on all the time, and then
we'd go out in the grassy courtyard and talk about films,
share our ideas and help each other with our problems . . .
The studio people never go to the movies. Sometimes they're
forced to sit through the films they're producing, but basically they don't care about movies. We do. We all went to film
school because we love movies, and we know what we need
to make them.'

Charles Weber, who was brought in to run the business,
persuaded Lucas that the Egg Company, as ILM was facetiously nicknamed, should stay in Los Angeles. But the entire
scheme began to be a huge financial strain: in the 1980s,
Lucasfilm cost $9 million a year to run. One day Weber
suggested that Skywalker Ranch was too great a drain on the
company. Lucas saw straightaway that Weber was missing the
point. He closed down the LA office and brought some of the
employees north. Lucas had regained control of Lucasfilm,
whose only constant profit came from merchandising.

8 Return of the Jedi

In his own individual way George Lucas remained true to his first love of film. In 1980, for example, he had persuaded Francis Coppola to join him in executive producing Akira Kurosawa's next picture, *Kagemusha*, and had chivvied Fox to put up half the money to finish the film. *Kagemusha* subsequently won the Palme d'Or at the Cannes Film Festival.

The next year he oversaw Lawrence Kasdan make the steamy film noir thriller *Body Heat*, having first convinced Alan Ladd of the first-time director's talents. Although he was paid $250,000 and given five per cent of its profits, Lucas kept his name off the film – ever the political pragmatist, he was concerned that the decidedly adult content of *Body Heat* could interfere with the more family-orientated mood that surrounded the image and brand name of Lucasfilm.

After all, there was a larger work to be completed: the final film in the *Star Wars* trilogy. Following the success of *Raiders of the Lost Ark*, George Lucas wanted Steven Spielberg to direct the third *Star Wars* film. His friend, however, was unavailable. Irvin Kershner, he had learned early on in the *Empire* shoot, was too intellectual a director, endlessly open to debate about

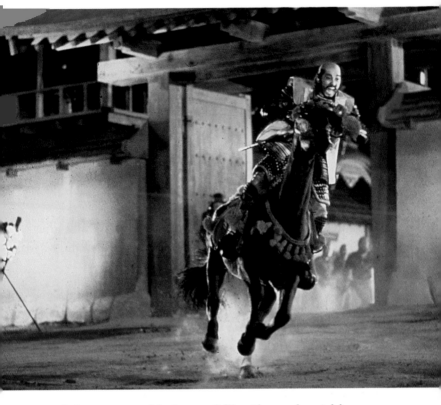

Remaining true to his love of film throughout his career, Lucas persuaded Francis Coppola to join him in producing Akira Kurosawa's Kagemusha.

the course of the plot and characterization. What Lucas really
needed was someone he felt he could control. 'He wanted
to hire a director who would be creative,' said Gary Kurtz –
who was not entirely unbiased as he had been dumped from
the Lucasfilm camp as a sacrificial victim after *Empire* had
raced over budget – 'but did everything exactly the way he
wanted it.'

Checking out available possibilities, Lucas came across
Richard Marquand, a Welshman in his early forties who had
been educated at Cambridge university. Marquand had
directed a popular television series, *The Search for the Nile*.
He had followed it up with *The Legacy*, a loony English-
country-house horror film starring Katherine Ross, and *The
Eye of the Needle*, a much better Second World War spy
thriller starring Donald Sutherland. (In 1985 Marquand was
to make a successful modern thriller, the Joe Eszterhas-
scripted *Jagged Edge*.) Marquand agreed not only to move
his family to California but to give Lucas all access during
post-production and during filming. He got the job.

We spent the day together [Lucas told Paul Scanlon in *Rolling
Stone* in August 1983]. It's a matter of getting to know the
person: his opinions on politics, life, philosophy and religion.
All these things will meld in the movie, so his sensibilities
have to be consistent with the sensibilities of the *Star Wars*
movies . . . I've got to find a director who's willing to give up
some of his domain to me and is willing to work with me and
accept the fact that he's essentially doing a movie that's been
established, that ultimately I'll have the final say . . .

I think, one, he has a great deal of enthusiasm for the
project: he liked *Star Wars*. Two, I think he wanted to work with

me, which helps. Finally, it's a very good career move for him. Obviously he's going to make an enormous amount of money, and he will be catapulted into the top directors thing and his salary will skyrocket. Then there's that practical side to it, too. It's a good job. It's a two-year job, but it's a good job. It's more than you can say about most movies.

Things had changed: George Lucas wrote the first draft for *Return of the Jedi* in four weeks, but then he asked Lawrence Kasdan to take over on the script. In this third film in the *Star Wars* trilogy would be the resolution of the problems created in the darker second film – the three films in the trilogy may be seen as the three acts that make up a classic Aristotelian drama. Soon Kasdan was locked away in long sessions with Richard Marquand. During a *Jedi* script conference, Lucas told Kasdan: 'The whole emotion I am trying to get at the end of this film is for you to be emotionally and spiritually uplifted and to feel absolutely good about life. That is the greatest thing that we could ever possibly do.'

And the plot emerged: Han Solo is freed by Princess Leia and Luke Skywalker, assisted by Lando Calrissian, from Jabba the Hutt and the carbonite in which he had been frozen; then the three hero figures head for the imperial bunker on the moon of Endor, from where the new Death Star is being controlled. On the way they encounter a new race of creatures, the Ewoks, tree-dwelling teddy bears (Lucas had thought up the idea of cut-down Chewbaccas) who become their allies.

Lucas's quality control never lapsed: only sixty of the hundreds of creatures manufactured at the Monster Factory made it as far as the film. The idea for the Ewoks, Lucas told

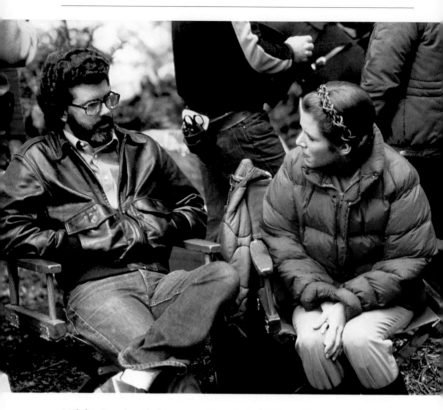

With Carrie Fisher on the set of The Return of the Jedi. **'It's as fast as you can make it and still tell a comprehensible story,' said Lucas.**

Scanlon, was 'just a short Wookie . . . they evolved and started getting cute. Dare to be cute. The worst we could do is get criticized for it . . . A lot of people are going to be offended by Ewoks. A lot of people say the films are just an excuse for merchandising: "Lucas just decided to cash in on the teddy bear." Well, it's not a great thing to cash in on, because there are lots of teddy bears marketed, so you don't have anything that's unique. If I were designing something original as a market item, I could probably do a lot better.'

But he made no bones about how essential marketing and merchandising were to Lucasfilm and its subsidiaries: 'We market everything in the movie. That's what keeps funding the other things we do – the computer research and all the other things. Again, people tend to look at merchandising as an evil thing. But ultimately, a lot of fun things come out of it, and at the same time, it pays for the overhead of the company and everybody's salary.'

The three principal characters were all six years older: Harrison Ford argued strongly that Han Solo should die at the end of the film. Lucas would not agree: he felt that it would ruin the ending of what was intended to be a positive film. Wasn't Ford's suggestion an indication that he had outgrown the *Star Wars* films? *Raiders of the Lost Ark* and *Blade Runner*, in which he also starred, had been superior pictures cinematically.

Carrie Fisher, meanwhile, was going through troubled times: she had been in a relationship with the singer-songwriter Paul Simon for seven years before marrying him. Then, after eleven months, the marriage had broken up.

Mark Hamill, meanwhile, had tried in vain to escape

Lucasfilm, discovering that he was so typecast as Luke Skywalker that he was virtually unemployable elsewhere.

Elstree aside, further locations were sought out for the January 1982 beginning of shooting. Buttercup Valley, near Yuma, Arizona, had the right sand dunes for another world. And the giant redwood forest at Crescent City, on the California/Oregon border, became Endor. At the time it was the largest film set ever built on location.

> You look at the Jabba the Hutt scene in *Return of the Jedi* [Lucas told Paul Scanlon] and say, 'Oh, that's what he wanted the cantina in *Star Wars* to be.' Or you look at the end battle, and you say, 'Oh, that's what the end battle was supposed to be in the first one.' But we couldn't have done this movie then. I mean, it just was not humanly possible or even financially possible. So a lot of these things I have finally worked out. I finally got the end battle the way I wanted it, I got the ground battle that I wanted, I got the monsters the way I wanted them.

During the making of *Star Wars*, Lucas's constant refrain on the film's aesthetics had been 'Faster – more intense.' On *Return of the Jedi* – known for some time as *Revenge of the Jedi* – this philosophy would seem to have reached fulfilment: the pace of *Return of the Jedi* is far closer to that of *Raiders of the Lost Ark* than to that of *Star Wars* or *The Empire Strikes Back*. In the *Star Wars* space battle the ships move slowly, continuity is virtually non-existent, and there are never more than two or three ships in a shot: in *Return of the Jedi* the storm of fighter aircraft is constructed from sixty-seven layers of film. 'It's as fast as you can make it and still tell a comprehensible story,' said Lucas to Scanlon. '*Jedi* is almost incomprehensible in certain areas. It's designed more for kids. It's sort of natural to the way I feel about things. I think it's the most emotional of the three films; at least it is for me. The end of a story, where everything comes together, is always the most emotional part.' And of that final battle in *Return of the Jedi*, he said to Scanlon:

It was designed for all the stories to come together. Stylistically, all the films are designed to have a big climax, and this one's sort of got everything in it. When we started, we said, 'Okay, now we're gonna do it the way we always wanted to do it. We've got the money, we've got the knowledge – this is it.'. . .

Whatever little event in history that *Star Wars* is going to be, at least it's done. If people want to look at it, they can look at the whole piece. That dumb screenplay I first wrote ten years ago is at least finished. It's all in a movie now. I was always contemplating rewriting the story, making it into more, because it was originally written as just a simple thing. It wasn't meant to be the giant phenomenon it turned out to be. You say, 'Well, now is this gonna live up to the phenomenon?' But I ultimately decided to stick with it and say, 'Look, that was the way it was written ten years ago, and this is where I was coming from. If it's not good enough, then tough luck.' You have to sort of have that attitude. For better or worse, I like it.

Released 25 May 1983, six years to the day after *Star Wars*, *Return of the Jedi* showed that the phenomenon indicated no signs of waning. Queues began forming eight days before *Jedi* opened. It proved to be even more successful than *The Empire Strikes Back*, becoming the third most successful film of all time, behind *Star Wars* and *E.T.*

But the film did not have unanimously favourable reviews. The New York critics were split: ten in favour, seven against, with those against, such as Pauline Kael, branding it a merchandising vehicle; or insisting that the human actors were overwhelmed by special effects. All the same, there was the usual rush of figures that accompanied the release of a *Star Wars* movie: on 25 May the film set an opening-day record of $6.2 million; the following Sunday it established a single-day record of $8.4 million; in week one *Return of the Jedi* pulled in $45.3 million; by mid-June it had grossed $70 million.

In that August 1983 interview with Paul Scanlon in *Rolling Stone*, Lucas had spoken in glowing terms of his relationship with Marcia Lucas: 'Being married to somebody in the film business helps. She worked on this film, and she worked on a number of the other films. There's a collaboration; we'd never have been able to survive otherwise. I don't know that many people in the film business who have managed to make it work. It's been very hard on Marcia, living with somebody who is constantly in agony, uptight and worried, off in never-never land.'

As is so often the case with event-pegged publicity, the interview had been conducted in advance of the premiere of *Return of the Jedi*. In the film Luke Skywalker works out what may loosely be termed as his 'father problem' – in other words, George Lucas' 'father problem'. But there was a sad irony to this: for in so doing had Lucas been neglecting any similar difficulties he had experienced with his female archetype?

A week after *Return of the Jedi* was released, Lucas held a staff meeting at Skywalker Ranch. With tears in his eyes, he announced that he and Marcia were to divorce.

9 Doom, Crusade and Star Wars to Come

His divorce sent George Lucas into 'a seven-year tailspin', as he later admitted to the *New York Times*. Although Lucasfilm and its associated companies were not affected by the resulting settlement with Marcia, he lost much of his personal fortune. *Star Wars*, however, had given him one of the definitive American movie empires, by now seemingly unstoppable in its snowballing course.

Although he had intended to take a two-year sabbatical after the completion of the *Star Wars* trilogy ('Suddenly my life is going to be mine. It's not going to be owned by Luke Skywalker and his friends,' he had declared to Paul Scanlon), the crisis in his personal life pushed him back into work. Even before *Return of the Jedi* hit the screens, he had been location scouting in Sri Lanka with Steven Spielberg, preparatory to setting up the shoot for the film that would become known as *Indiana Jones and the Temple of Doom*. For this movie the script had been written by Lucas' old friends Willard Huyck and Gloria Katz, who had put a final spin on the *Star Wars* dialogue and turned in a final draft of *American Graffiti*. Fearful that Spielberg might back out of his commitment to direct the movie, Lucas had impressed upon them the need to get a script to him as fast as possible.

Like the second *Star Wars* film, this second of what had become a planned *Indiana Jones* trilogy was – at Lucas's urging – by far the darkest of the three movies. Released in 1984, it was another enormous hit. Perhaps, as the critic David Thomson has suggested, Lucas's work was becoming a testament to the principle that American pictures are produced, not directed.

Like Woody Allen, the man who kicked *Star Wars* into touch with *Annie Hall* during the Academy Awards in 1978, George Lucas is never satisfied with a film that he has finished, and for the same reasons: he has always thought that it could have been so much more, that there was always a significant gap between the original idea and what finally appeared. But in this expression of discontent, Lucas is uttering a mythical tale of his own: the artist's quest for perfection, for the matching of the idea and its expression. 'Each film has accomplishments that I like. It's not that I didn't like the movies, but that if I look at them now, each one falls a bit short of what I had hoped it to be – because I guess I either set my sights a little bit lower, or we actually do get a little bit better.'

Whatever he may have thought of the films (and television series) he was about to release, Lucas' beliefs were about to be tested. Lucasfilm was now as financially secure as it could hope to be – although, allowing for the exigencies of box-office fate, this might mean very little. But none of the films it would produce for the next five years would come anywhere close to the epic box-office standards established by the *Star Wars* and *Indiana Jones* series.

Much of the time, however, it seemed Lucas would hardly expect them to, and that he was simply paying respect to other fine film artists, as with Paul Schrader's *Mishima: A Life in Four Chapters* in 1985 and his mentor Haskell Wexler's *Latino* the same year. The next year brought *Howard the Duck*, directed by Willard Huyck and a financial flop. But 1988 saw Lucasfilm sponsoring Godfrey Reggio's wonderful, innovative, determinedly uncommercial *Powaqqatsi*; and Francis Coppola's inspired but fiscally doomed *Tucker: The Man and His Dream*, the story of the man who took on the might of the Motown automobile manufacturers. 'I've dealt with things like *Tucker*, which, in terms of connecting with an audience, don't work, but I've never made a movie I'm not happy with,' Lucas stated in a biographical television programme in the BBC's *Omnibus* series.

'George', Coppola informed the same programme, 'was one of the most talented American film directors of that time and somehow, because of *Star Wars*, we were deprived of those movies he was going to make. Instead, we have an enormous industrial marketing complex.'

Faring far better at the box office that year for Lucasfilm was Ron Howard's *Willow*, which re-worked many of the mythological themes of the *Star Wars* trilogy. 'There were definitely some parallels between some of the characters and situations of *Star Wars* and *Willow*,' said Howard, 'and I was working against that. But it wasn't a problem, because the *Star Wars* characters weren't really original either – they were an acknowledgement and all he had done was put them in this sci-fi world. And all we were doing was creating this world of magic and sword and sorcery.'

On *American Graffiti*, Lucas remembered, Ron Howard was never without an 8mm camera: 'He was always running around taking movies of us making the movie and saying how he was going to film school and become a director . . . These films, I think, deal with some very important issues of today – Good versus Evil, how to conduct yourself in society . . . It's just that they're not talking about them directly. *Willow* is about people and ideas. The underlying issues, the psychological motives are the same as in all my movies: personal responsibility and friendship, the importance of living a compassionate life as opposed to a passionate or selfish life. These issues are, I think, very relevant to what you can be today.'

It was down to *Indiana Jones and the Last Crusade*, the third film in the series, to return Lucasfilm to the world of box-office smashes. In this film, in which Jones is joined by his father, played by Sean Connery, the quest continues for the Holy Grail, with evil Nazis again the enemy. Superior to the second movie, the film was arguably a match for *Raiders of the Lost Ark*.

Spielberg defined his mission perfectly, interlocking his personal skills with those of ILM's special-effects department. Visually, the film was extraordinary: the apparently impossible shot of a German gunner flying in locked focus towards the camera; the extraordinary scene, stripped down to symbolic essentials, in which our resourceful hero battles a tank from horseback; the Leap of Faith in which the ledge across an immense ravine is hidden by spatial distortion.

What is remarkable about the completion of the first *Star Wars* trilogy is that George Lucas could have had the ambition, the steely determination and the nerve to conceive and carry it out.

'The three movies were originally one idea, one big story, one screenplay – a 300-page script, a six-hour-and-fifteen-minute movie,' he said. 'The first one is a very elaborate introduction of the characters. The second obviously sets everything up, and the third is the one that pays it off.'

Despite the colossal scale of his ambition, Lucas had played it all along one step at a time.

You know, *Star Wars* was a success, but I didn't have any idea then what was going on. I didn't know whether I was even going to be able to make the next two films. I had taken two-thirds of the original script and thrown it away. In my mind, I was saying, 'Gee, if this is really a big hit, then I can make a movie out of all the early material that I developed.' *Empire* and *Jedi* were what that first film was supposed to be. And after that, I can tell another story about what happens to Luke after this trilogy ends. All the prequel stories exist: where Darth Vader came from, the whole story about Darth and Ben Kenobi, and it all takes place before Luke was born. The other one – what happens to Luke afterwards – is much more ethereal. I have a tiny notebook full of notes on that. If I'm really ambitious, I could proceed to figure out what would have happened to Luke.

But, George Lucas said, he would only make the prequel films if they could be made more cheaply and simply. 'I couldn't afford to make another like *Jedi*. I wouldn't take the risk. Inflation in films is astronomical . . . I think if we started the next series, we would probably try to do all three of them at once.'

And then . . . *Nothing!*

Or so it seemed. In fact, Lucas was quietly active all the time, through ILM his influence on contemporary cinema larger than when he was making and releasing the *Star Wars* and *Indiana Jones* trilogy: *Jurassic Park*, for example, being dependent on Industrial Light and Magic. And it was only after ILM showed they could render a credible tornado that a studio backed *Twister*.

In fact, at first directly through his own work and then via the unparalleled efficiency and influence of ILM, George Lucas has dictated for two decades the essential broad notion of what is cinema. The list of hits – films that could not have otherwise existed – with which ILM is associated is staggering and shows the full influence of George Lucas on modern cinema. It includes *Ghost*, *Terminator 2: Judgement Day*, *E.T.*, *Poltergeist*, the *Star Trek* series, *Out of Africa*, *The Money Pit*, *Labyrinth*, *The Golden Child*, *The Witches of Eastwick*, *Empire of the Sun*, *Who Framed Roger Rabbit?*, *The Last Temptation of Christ*, *Field of Dreams*, *Ghostbusters II*, *The Abyss*, *Back to the Future II* and *III*, *Always*, Akira Kurosawa's *Dreams*, *The Hunt for Red October*, *Die Hard 2*, *The Godfather III*, *The Doors*, *Backdraft*, *The Rocketeer* and *Hook*.

Special effects and narrative had become inextricably interwoven, the effects becoming part of the content. And ILM had become an intriguing blend of aesthetic impact and business success. George Lucas himself said, 'Special effects are just a tool . . . without a story, it's a pretty boring thing.

In 1996 an announcement came forth from Lucasfilm headquarters: the next year production would begin, at the new Millennium Studios in Leavesden, Hertfordshire, on the

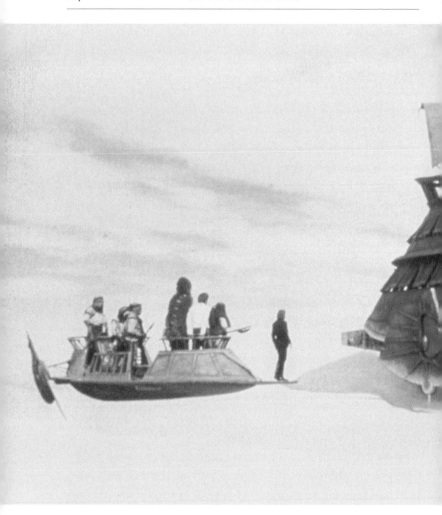

The 'restored' version of The Return of the Jedi**, released as a special edition with** Star Wars **and** The Empire Strikes Back**, in 1997. All three films had digitally cut footage and scenes added.**

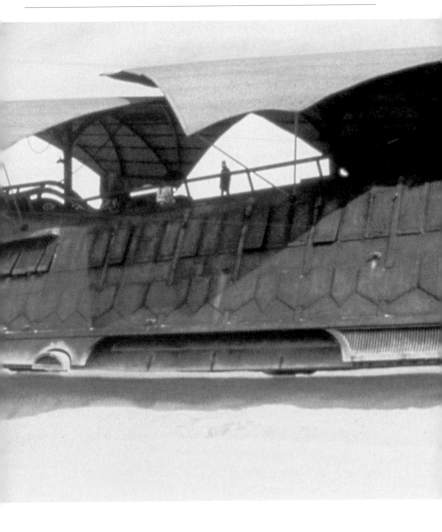

three *Star Wars* prequel films. From 1999 onwards these would appear at two-yearly intervals. Tellingly, we were told that Pepsi-Cola would finance them to the tune of roughly $2 billion.

What was more, the original *Star Wars* trilogy would be re-released from January 1997 onwards; this 'special edition' would have had cut footage digitally restored and, in certain (albeit minor) cases, scenes added.

By the time this re-cut version began to appear, the *Star Wars* trilogy already had earned $1.3 billion (mind you, this was less than half the $3 billion it had brought in from merchandising). The whims and fancies of succeeding years, however, meant that it was now a long while since *Star Wars* had been the top-earning picture of all time. On that opening weekend at the end of January 1997, however, Luke Skywalker and his friends once again turned everything on their head: the first weekend's box-office take was over $36 million (Lucas had predicted something in the $10 million range), and by the time it ended its run, *Star Wars* was once again the biggest earning film of all time – twenty years after its first release. (Although even in the market-led 1990s we always had to bear in mind that commercial success was not an *ipso facto* guarantee of quality. 'No matter how many billions of dollars *Star Wars* can earn, and no matter how valuable that franchise, it isn't worth a tenth of what he's worth and capable of doing as an artist,' said Francis Ford Coppola, the controversial artist to the last, commenting on the course of his friend's career.)

'The prequels will be a much darker and more complex set of films,' announced Rick McCallum, their producer. 'They hinge around the story of Anakim Skywalker, who is Darth

Vader. And we meet Anakim as a young boy, and we watch him become a Jedi knight, and watch him meet Obi-Wan, who becomes his mentor. But much more importantly, all of these films lead up to that crisis point in his life when he chooses the dark side.'

'You actually get the full story,' said Lucas to *Omnibus* about the prequel, 'and you're able to see them in context and you understand Vader's side of the story, which you haven't heard yet. Ultimately, with *Star Wars* the big chance I'm taking is I'm working on something I started on twenty years ago, and whether it will fit into the modern world marketing-wise I don't know. Fortunately I'm in the position where I don't have to worry too much.'

THE

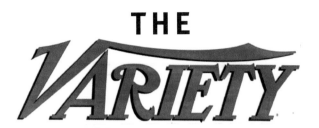

REVIEWS

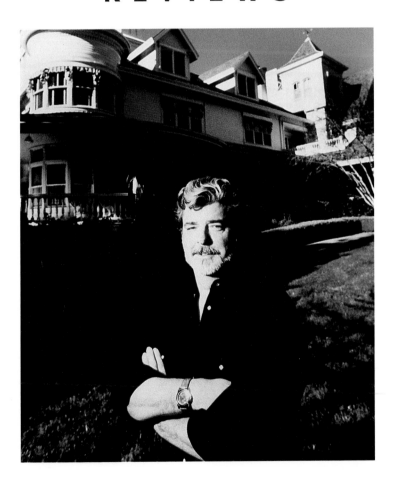

THX 1138

March 17, 1971

Abstract, handsomely stylistic but sluggish sci-fi drama about future enslavement by computer. Nixed b.o. at present, but could become a future buff class. Hollywood, March 9. (COLOR)

Warner Bros. release of an American Zoetrope production; executive producer, Francis Ford Coppola; produced by Lawrence Sturhahn. Directed by George Lucas. Screenplay, Lucas, Walter Murch, from a Lucas story; camera (Technicolor), Dave Meyers, Albert Kihn; editor, Lucas; music, Lalo Schifrin; art direction, Michael Haller; sound, Murch, Lou Yates, Jim Manson. Reviewed at Loews Hollywood, L.A., March 8, '71. (MPAA Rating: PG.) Running Time, 88 MINS.)

THX 1138	Robert Duvall
SEN	Donald Pleasence
SRT	Don Pedro Colley
LUH	Maggie McOmie
PTO	Ian Wolfe
NCH	Sid Haig
TWA	Marshall Efron
DWY	John Pearce
Police Robots	Johnny Weismuller, Jr.,
	Robert Feero
IMM	Irene Forrest
ELC	Claudette Bessing

"THX 1138" is a psychedelic science fiction horror story about some future civilization regimented into computer-programmed slavery. Likely not to be an artistic or commercial success in its own time, the American Zoetrope (Francis Ford Coppola) group production just might in time become a classic of stylistic, abstract cinema. Story has some disturbingly plausible overtones, but only a portion of the esoteric audience may turn onto the Warner Bros. release at this time. Heavy exploitation may yield mixed results.

Film is a feature-length expansion of George Lucas' student film which won kudos some three years ago. In that brief form, the story of one man's determination to crash out of his wordly prison was exciting; the expansion by director-editor Lucas with Walter Murch succeeds in fleshing out the environment, but falls behind in constructing a plot line to sustain interest. Robert Duvall heads cast as the defector after his mate Maggie McOmie is programmed into the cell of Donald Pleasence, a corrupt computer technician. Don Pedro Colley is another fugitive, who helps Duvall reach his freedom. Dave Meyers and Albert Kihn photographed superbly the extremely handsome futuristic physical values designed by Michael Haller. Lalo Schifrin's score is outstanding. Murch is credited with the excellent sound montages which blend some familiar recorded-announcement cliches with the low-key terror of an Orwellian "Alice In Wonderland", where drug use and sexual suppression are mandatory, and the major crimes are drug evasion and sex relations. With political paternalism rampant at both extremes of the spectrum, Lucas is onto something. In any case, we'll know for sure in about a generation.

Murf.

AMERICAN GRAFFITI

June 20, 1973

Outstanding evocation of '50s teenagers, told with humor and heart. Strong outlook. Hollywood, June 16. (COLOR)

Universal Pictures release, produced by Francis Ford Coppola; co-producer, Gary Kurtz. Directed by George Lucas. Screenplay, Lucas, Gloria Katz, Willard Huyck; camera (Technicolor), Haskell Wexler; editors, Verna Fields, Marcia Lucas; music supervision, Karin Green; art direction, Dennis Clark; set decoration, Douglas Freeman; sound, Walter Murch, Arthur Rochester; asst. director, Ned Kopp. Reviewed at Directors' Guild of America, L.A., June 15, '73. (MPAA Rating: PG.) Running Time: 109 MINS.

Curt	Richard Dreyfuss
Steve	Ronny Howard
John	Paul Le Mat
Terry	Charlie Martin Smith
Laurie	Cindy Williams
Debbie	Candy Clark
Carol	Mackenzie Phillips
Disc Jockey	Wolfman Jack
Bob Falfa	Harrison Ford
Gang Members	Bo Hopkins,
	Manuel Padilla Jr., Beau Gentry
Rock Band	Flash Cadillac and the
	Continental Kids
Teacher	Terry McGovern
Policeman	Jim Bohan
Wendy	Debbie Celiz
Blonde in Car	Suzanne Somers
Vagrant	George Meyer
Thief	James Cranna
Liquor Store Clerk	William Niven

Of all the youth-themed nostalgia films in the past couple of years, George Lucas' "American Graffiti" is among the very best to date. Set in 1962 but reflecting the culmination of the '50s, the film is a most vivid recall of teenage attitudes and mores, told with outstanding empathy and compassion through an exceptionally talented cast of relatively new players. The Universal release, filmed in small towns north of San Francisco, is first-rate Americana which should strike its most responsive chord among audiences of 40 years of age and under, though older filmgoers certainly should enjoy it also.

Francis Ford Coppola was the nominal producer, and Gary Kurtz was co-producer. The superior original screenplay, in which the predominant comedy values are deftly supported by underlying serious elements of adolescent maturation, was written by director Lucas in collaboration with Gloria Katz and Willard Huyck. This is Lucas' second feature; his first, "THX 1138," was a futuristic socio-political drama, not quite the total fantasy many might have thought it to be.

"American Graffiti" occupies that very lonely ground between the uptight misunderstood teenage mellers of its era, and the beach-party fluff on which American International held the only successful patents. Its milieu is the accumulated junk and materialism of the Eisenhower years, an endowment of tin theology and synthetic values which, in younger generations, sowed the seeds of an incoherent unrest that would mature violently a decade later.

Design consultant Al Locatelli, art director Dennis Clark and set director

Douglas Freeman have brilliantly reconstructed the fabric and texture of the time, while Walter Murch's outstanding sound collage – an unending stream of early rock platter hits – complements in the aural department. "Visual consultant" (read: cameraman) Haskell Wexler has done an excellent job in capturing the mood, refreshingly devoid of showoff lensing gimmicks. Even the limitations of the now-rarely used Techniscope anamorphic process contribute an artful touch of grainy, sweaty reality.

Against this chrome and neon backdrop is told the story of one long summer night in the lives of four school chums: Richard Dreyfuss, on his last night before leaving for an eastern college; Ronny Howard, less willing to depart the presence of Cindy Williams; Charlie Martin Smith, a bespectacled fumbler whose misadventures with pubescent swinger Candy Clark are as touching as they are hilarious; and Paul Le Mat, 22 years old on a birth certificate but still strutting as he did four years earlier.

Mackenzie Phillips, in real life the 12-year-old daughter of composer John Phillips, is sensational in film debut as a likeable brat whom Le Mat cannot shake from his car. Harrison Ford is a hot-rodder whose drag-race challenge to Le Mat provides a discreetly violent climax to the story's restless night. Bo Hopkins leads a gang of toughs, and longtime deejay Wolfman Jack is heard regularly on the sound collage, and appears briefly in a scene with Dreyfuss.

There is brilliant interplaying, and underplaying, of script, performers and direction which will raise howls of laughter from audiences, yet never descends

on the screen to overdone mugging, pratfall and other heavy-handed devices normally employed. Some petting scenes get their point across without the patronizing voyeurisms so often found in nostalgia pix. The filmmakers' hearts obviously were with their characters all the way. Lucas has done a truly masterful job.

Murch's sound track uses about 40 platter hits, not all of which were precisely contemporaneous but no harm done. Film opens with Bill Hayley's "Rock Around The Clock," which serves Lucas as well now as it did Richard Brooks in 1955 in that never-to-be-forgotten whammo main title of "The Blackboard Jungle." Karin Green was music coordinator. Kim Fowley produced the two original recordings for the film, done by Flash Cadillac and The Continental Kids, playing a local rock band engaged for a freshman hop.

In such a meritorious filmmaking ensemble, lots more people contributed: hair stylists Gerry Leetch and Betty Iverson; editors (to 109 minutes) Verna Fields and Marcia Lucas; operating cameramen Ron Eveslage and Jan D'Alquen; costume designer Aggie Guerard Rodgers; choreographer Tony Basil; production sound recorder Arthur Rochester; sound editor James Nelson; and casting supervisors Fred Roos and Mike Fenton.

Without exception, all players fit perfectly into the concept and execution, and all the young principals and featured players have a bright and lengthy future. And so does Lucas. "American Graffiti" is one of those rare films which can be advanced in any discussion of the

superiority of films over live performances; the latter can vary from show to
show, but if you get it right on film,
you've got it forever.

Murf.

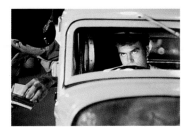

STAR WARS

May 25, 1977

Outstanding adventure-fantasy. All-age
appeal. Huge outlook. Hollywood, May 19.
(COLOR)

**Twentieth Century-Fox release, produced
by Gary Kurtz. Written and directed by
George Lucas, Camera (Technicolor;
prints by Deluxe), Gilbert Taylor; second
unit camera, Carroll Ballard, Rick
Clemente, Robert Dalva, Tak Fujimoto;
editors, Paul Hirsch, Marcia Lucas,
Richard Chew; music, John Williams;
production design, John Barry; art direc-
tion, Norman Reynolds, Leslie Dilley; set
decoration, Roger Christian; sound
(Dolby), Don McDougal, Bob Minkler, Ray
West, Mike Minkler, Les Fresholtz,
Richard Portman, Derek Ball, Stephen
Katz; costumes-wardrobe, John Mollo,
Ron Beck; stunt coordinator, Peter
Diamond. Reviewed at 20th-Fox Studios,
L.A., May 19, 1977 (MPAA rating: PG.)
Running time: 121 MINS.**

Additional Production Credits

Special photographic effects supervisor,
John Dykstra; special production and
mechanical effects supervisor, John Stears;
production supervisor, Robert Watts;
production illustration, Ralph McQuarrie;
special dialogue and sound effects, Ben
Burtt; sound editors, Sam Shaw, Robert R.
Rutledge, Gordon Davidson, Gene Corso.

Miniature And Optical Effects Credits

First camera, Richard Edlund; composite
optical photography, Robert Blalack
(Praxis); optical photography, Paul Roth;
animation and rotoscope design, Adam
Beckett; stop-motion animation, Jon Berg,
Philip Tippet.

Luke Skywalker	Mark Hamill
Han Solo	Harrison Ford
Princess Organa [sic]	Carrie Fisher
Grand Moff Tarkin	Peter Cushing
Ben Kenobi	Alec Guinness
C3PO	Anthony Daniels
R2D2	Kenny Baker
Chewbacca	Peter Mayhew
Lord Darth Vader	David Prowse
Uncle Owen Lars	Phil Brown
Aunt Beru Lars	Shelagh Fraser
Chief Jawa	Jack Purvis
Rebel Generals	Alex McCrindle, Eddie Byrne
Imperial Military Chiefs	Don Henderson, Richard LeParmentier, Leslie Schofield
Rebels	Drewe Henley, Dennis Lawson, Garrick Hagon, Jack Klaff, William Hootkins, Angus McInnis, Jeremy Sinden, Graham Ashley

"Star Wars" is a magnificent film. George Lucas set out to make the biggest possible adventure-fantasy out of his memories of serials and older action epics, and he has succeeded brilliantly. Lucas and producer Gary Kurtz assembled an enormous technical crew, drawn from the entire Hollywood production pool of talent, and the results equal the genius of Walt Disney, Willis O'Brien and other justifiably famous practitioners of what Irwin Allen calls "movie magic." The 20th-Fox release is also loaded with boxoffice magic, with potent appeal across the entire audience spectrum.

The story is an engaging space adventure which takes itself seriously while occasionally admitting an affectionate poke at the genre. The most immediate frame of reference is a Flash Gordon film, but it's more than that; it's an Errol Flynn escapist adventure, and befitting that, composer John Williams and orchestrator Herbert W. Spencer have supplied a rousing score worthy of Korngold and Steiner.

Like a breath of fresh air, "Star Wars" sweeps away the cynicism that has in recent years obscured the concepts of valor, dedication and honor. Make no mistake – this is by no means a "children's film" with all the derogatory overtones that go with that description. This is instead a superior example of what only the screen can achieve, and closer to home, it is another affirmation of what only Hollywood can put on a screen.

In casting his principals, Lucas chose three not-so-familiar faces, all young, talented and designed to make the story one of people, not of garish gadgetry. The superb balance of technology and human drama is one of the many achievements; one identifies with the characters and accepts, as do they, the intriguing intergalactic world in which they live.

Carrie Fisher, previously in a small role in "Shampoo," is delightful as the regal, but spunky princess on a rebel planet who has been kidnapped by Peter Cushing, would-be ruler of the universe. Mark Hamill, previously a tv player, is excellent as a farm boy who sets out to rescue Fisher in league with Alec Guinness, last survivor of a band of noble knights. Harrison Ford, previously in Lucas' "American Graffiti" and Francis Coppola's "The Conversation," is outstanding as a likeable mercenary pilot who joins our friends with his pal Peter Mayhew, a quasi-monkey creature with blue eyes whom Fisher calls "a walking rug."

Both Guinness and Cushing bring the right measure of majesty to their opposite characters. One of Cushing's key aides is David Prowse, destined to a fatal duel with Guinness, with whom he shares mystical powers. Prowse's face is never seen, concealed as it is behind frightening black armor. James Earl Jones, unbilled, provides a note of sonorous menace as Prowse's voice, Anthony Daniels and Kenny Baker play a Mutt-and-Jeff team of kooky robots.

The heroes and the heavies joust through an exciting series of confrontations, replete with laser guns and other futuristic equipment, building suspense towards the climactic destruction of Cushing's war-mongering planet. Several chase and escape sequences are likely to stimulate spontaneous audience applause.

Lucas is no credit hog, and all contributions are acknowledged on the end titles, bearing all the names listed above as well as assistants in various categories. The film opens after the 20th logo, with the type of receding crawl that Flash Gordon fans will recognize. Locations in Tunisia, Death Valley, Guatemala and Africa were utilized, and interiors were shot at EMI's British studios where the terrific score was also recorded. But the technical effects work was all done here. Technicolor did the production color work, and DeLuxe the prints. Use of Dolby sound enhances the overall impact.

Lucas' first feature, "THX-1138," was also futuristic in tone, but there the story emphasis was on machines controlling man. But in "Star Wars" the people remain the masters of the hardware, thereby strik-

ing a more resonant note of empathy and hope. This is the kind of film in which an audience, first entertained, can later walk out feeling good all over.

Murf.

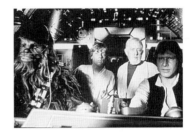

MORE AMERICAN GRAFFITI

July 25, 1979

Ambitious sequel over-reaches itself, to boxoffice detriment. Hollywood, July 19. (COLOR)

A Universal Pictures release of a Lucasfilm Ltd. production. Produced by Howard Kazanjian. Exec producer, George Lucas. Directed by B.W.L. Norton. Features entire cast. Screenplay, Norton, based on characters created by Lucas, Gloria Katz, Willard Huyck; camera (Technicolor), Caleb Deschanel; editor, Tina Hirsch; art direction, Ray Storey; sound (Dolby Stereo), David McMillan; costume design, Agnes Rodgers; set decoration, Doug Van Koss: assistant director, Thomas Lofaro. Reviewed at Goldwyn Theatre, BevHills. July 19. '79. (MPAA Rating: PG) Running time: 111 MINS.

Debbie Dunham	Candy Clark
Little Joe	Bo Hopkins
Steve Bolander	Ron Howard
John Milner	Paul Le Mat
Carol/Rainbow	Mackenzie Phillips
Terry The Toad	Charles Martin Smith
Laurie Bolander	Cindy Williams
Eva	Anna Bjorn
Major Creech	Richard Bradford
Ralph	John Brent
Newt	Scott Glenn
Sinclair	James Houghton
Lance	John Lansing
Beckwith	Ken Place
Teensa	Mary Kay Place
Andy Henderson	Will Seltzer
Felix	Ralph Wilcox

"More American Graffiti" may be one of the most innovative and ambitious films of the last five years, but by no means is it one of the most successful. In trying to follow the success of George Lucas' immensely popular 1973 hit, writer-director B.W.L. Norton overloads the sequel with four wholly different cinematic styles to carry forward the lives of "American Graffiti's" original cast. Initial returns should be very strong, on title lure alone, but repeat biz looks to be shallow.

While dazzling to the eye, the flirtation with split-screen, anamorphic, 16m and 1:85 screen sizes does not justify itself in terms of the film's content. What Norton and producer Howard Kazanjian are attempting, and what a variety of technicians pull off flawlessly, is daring, but ultimately pointless.

There's a lot going on in "More American Graffiti", as Norton takes the characters (minus a few exceptions) created by Lucas, Gloria Katz and Willard Huyck, and advances them two, three, four and five years into their future.

Paul Le Mat's still rooted in the early '60s, drag-racing and pursuing an Icelandic beauty (Anna Bjorn) with whom he's no more successful in communicating than he was in the original with Mackenzie Phillips. Charles Martin Smith and Bo Hopkins are assigned to a helicopter unit in Vietnam, while Candy Clark and Phillips have gone the flower power route in San Francisco. As expected, Ron Howard and Cindy Williams have married.

Part of Norton's presumed goal, of course, is to show how the 1960s fractured and split apart, and that the cohesiveness that marked Lucas' (and the participants' lives) film is now dissipated, as characters branch out, and in some instances, are snuffed out.

But without a dramatic glue to hold the disparate story elements together, "Graffiti" is too disorganized for its own good, and the cross-cutting between different film styles only accentuates the problem.

Otherwise, Lucasfilm Ltd. has amassed an extraordinary cast and crew that succeeds in almost snatching victory from the jaws of defeat. The aural counterpoint via period recordings that virtually changed the conception of film soundtracks is again employed to excellent, if more downbeat, effect by music editor Gene Finley, supervising sound editor Ben Burtt and re-recordist Bill Varney, Steve Maslow and Greg Landaker.

Work of cinematographer Caleb Deschanel, and optical coordinators Peter Donen, and Bill Lindemann, is extraordinary in meshing the four film sizes, which are beautifully handled in effortless segues. Especially noteworthy are the Vietnam sequences, filmed in Central California, and almost as impressive as some of the "Apocalypse Now" footage.

Smith tops the performers as the likeable klutz, unable to get himself wounded and sent home even in the midst of the Vietnam War. Clark carries off her psychedelic scenes with panache, and Howard and Williams sparkle as the young marrieds force to confront a changing society.

Bjorn is terrif as Le Mat's uncomprehending Venus, and Le Mat himself shows remarkable continuity in characterization, especially after a six-year layoff. Supporting players are uniformly well-chosen, with Scott Glenn and Ralph Wilcox very good as rock band members.

Mary Kay Place as Bjorn's girlfriend, and Ralph Place as Le Mat's competitive buddy. Richard Dreyfuss, only cast principal not to return, is sorely missed, but Harrison Ford shows up in an unbilled cameo as a motorcycle cop. Phillips, one of the first film's most delightful characters, gets short shrift in this version.

Rest of thesping and tech work is all more than acceptable, but doesn't help. "More American Graffiti" offers conclusive proof that in the case of sequels, less can be more.

Poll.

THE EMPIRE STRIKES BACK

May 14, 1980

The Force Is Still With It. Hollywood, May 7. (COLOR)

A 20th Century-Fox release, produced by Gary Kurtz. Exec producer, George Lucas. Directed by Irvin Kershner. Screenplay, Leigh Brackett and Lawrence Kasdan, based on story by Lucas; camera (Rank Film Color/DeLuxe prints), Peter Suschitzy; editor, Paul Hirsch; sound (Dolby Stereo), Peter Sutton; special visual effects, Brian Johnson, Richard Edlund; associate producers, Robert Watts, James Bloom; art direction, Leslie Dilley, Harry Lange, Alan Tomkins; set decoration, Michael Ford; make-up and special creature design, Stuart Freeborn; costumes, John Mollo; design consultant, Ralph McQuarrie; music, John Williams. Reviewed at 20th Century-Fox, May 7, 1980. (MPAA rating: PG) Running time: 124 MINS.

Luke Skywalker	Mark Hamill
Hans Solo	Harrison Ford
Princess Leia	Carrie Fisher
Darth Vader	David Prowse
C3PO	Anthony Daniels
Chewbacca	Peter Mayhew
R2-D2	Kenny Baker
Yoda	Frank Oz
Lando Calrissian	Billy Dee Williams
Ben Kenobi	Alec Guinness

Other cast: Jeremy Bulloch, John Hollis, Jack Purvis, Des Webb, Kathryn Mullen, Clive Revill, Kenneth Colley, Julian Glover, Michael Sheard, Michael Culver, John Dicks, Milton Johns, Mark Jones, Oliver Maguire, Robin Scobey, Bruce Boa, Christopher Malcolm, Dennis Lawson, Richard Oldfield, John Morton, Ian Liston, John Ratzenberger, Jack McKenzie, Jerry Harte, Norman Chancer, Norwich Duff, Ray Hassett, Brigitte Kahn, Burnell Tucker.

Additional Production Credits

Production supervisor, Bruce Sharman; studio second-unit direction, Harley Cokliss, John Barry; studio second-unit camera, Chris Menges; location second-unit direction, Peter MacDonald; location second-unit camera, Geoff Glover; assistant directors, David Tomblin, Dominic Fulford, Bill Westley, Ola Solum; mechanical effects supervision, Nick Allder; sound design, Ben Burtt.

Miniature and Optical Effects Unit Credits

Effects photography, Dennis Muren; optical photography, Bruce Nicholson; art direction-visual effects, Joe Johnston; stop motion animation, Jon Berg, Phil Tippet; matte painting, Harrison Ellenshaw; model maker, Lorne Peterson; animation and rotoscope, Peter Kuran; visual effects editing. Conrad Buff.

"The Empire Strikes Back" is a worthy sequel to "Star Wars," equal in both technical mastery and characterization, suffering only from the familiarity with the effects generated in the original and imitated too much by others. Only boxoffice question is how many earthly trucks it will take to carry the cash to the bank.

From the first burst of John Williams' powerful score and the receding opening title crawl, we are back in pleasant surroundings and anxious for a good time – like walking through the front gate of Disneyland, where good and evil are never confused and the righteous will always win.

This is exec producer George Lucas' world. Though he has turned the director's chair over to the capable Irvin Kershner and his typewriter to Leigh Brackett and Lawrence Kasdan, there are no recognizable deviations from the path marked by Lucas and producer Gary Kurtz.

Having already introduced their principal players, the filmmakers now have a chance to round them out, assisted again by good performances from Mark Hamill, Harrison Ford and Carrie Fisher. And even the ominous Darth Vader (David Prowse) is fleshed with new – and surprising – motivations. Killed in the original, Alec Guinness is limited to ghostly cameo.

Responding, too, to the audience's obvious affection for the non-human sidekicks, "Empire" makes full use of Chewbacca (Peter Mayhew), C3PO (Anthony Daniels) and R2D2 (Kenny Baker). Among the new characters, Billy Dee Williams gets a good turn as a duplicitous but likeable villain-ally and Frank Oz is fascinating as sort of a guru for the Force. How this dwarfish character was created and made to seem so real is a wonder, but it's only one of many visual marvels.

There are new creatures like the Tautaun on the ice planet Hoth and dreadful new mechanical menaces such as the giant four-legged, walking juggernauts, plus the usual array of motherships and fighter craft, odd space stations and asteroids.

But it's all believable given the premise, made the more enjoyable by Lucas' heavy borrowing – with a splashing new coat of sci-fi paint – from many basic film frameworks. The juggernaut attack on infantry in the trenches with fighter planes counterattacking overhead is straight out of every war film ever made.

Even more than before, Lucas and Kershner seem to be making the comparisons obvious. Vader's admirals look now even more dressed like Japanese admirals of the fleet intercut with Hammill's scrambling fighter pilots who wouldn't look too out of place on any Marine base today.

Oz's eerie jungle home would not confuse Tarzan and the carbon-freezing chamber that threatens Ford could be substituted for any alligator pit in a Lost Temple. Naturally, too, the laser saber battles of the first are back again even more, along with the wild-west shootouts and aerial dogfights.

At 124 minutes, "Empire" is only three minutes longer than its predecessor, but seems to be longer than that, probably because of the overfamiliarity with some of the space sequences and excessive saber duels between Vader and Hamill.

Reaching its finish, "Empire" blatantly sets up the third in the "Star Wars" trilogy, presuming the marketplace will signify its interest. It's a pretty safe presumption.

Har.

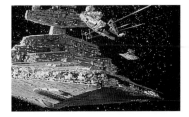

RAIDERS OF THE LOST ARK

Wednesday, June 10, 1981

Smashing adventure-fantasy that brings back the good old days. Major b.o. prospects. (COLOR)

A Paramount Pictures release of a Lucasfilm Ltd. Production. Produced by Frank Marshall. Executive producers, George Lucas, Howard Kazanjian. Directed by Steven Spielberg. Features entire cast. Screenplay, Lawrence Kasdan; story, Lucas, Philip Kaufman; associate producer, Robert Watts; camera (Metrocolor), Douglas Slocombe; music, John Williams; editor, Michael Kahn; production designer, Norman Reynolds; art direction, Leslie Dilley; visual effects supervisor, Richard Edlund. Reviewed at Paramount screening room, N.Y., June 2, 1981. (MPAA Rating: PG) Running time: 115 MINS.

Indy	Harrison Ford
Marion	Karen Allen
Dietrich	Wolf Kahler
Belloq	Paul Freeman
Toht	Ronald Lacey
Sallah	John Rhys-Davies
Brody	Denholm Elliott
Gobler	Anthony Higgins
Satipo	Alfred Molina
Barranca	Vic Tablian

"Raiders of the Lost Ark" is the stuff that raucous Saturday matinees at the local Bijou once were made of, a crackerjack fantasy-adventure that shapes its pulp sensibilities arid cliff-hanging serial origins into an exhilarating escapist entertainment that will have broad-based summer audiences in the palm of its hand. Even within this summer's hot competitive environment, boxoffice prospects are in the top rank.

Steeped in an exotic atmosphere of lost civilizations, mystical talismans, gritty mercenary adventurers, Nazi arch-villains and ingenious death at every turn, the film is largely patterned on the serials of the 1930s, with a large dollop of Edgar Rice Burroughs.

Story begins in 1936 as Indiana Jones (Harrison Ford), an archaeologist and university professor who's not above a little mercenary activity on the side, plunders a South American jungle tomb. Fending off an awesome array of deadly primitive booby-traps – ranging from light-sensitive poison darts and impaling spikes to legions of tarantulas – he secures a priceless golden Godhead, only to have it snatched away by longtime archaeological rival Paul Freeman, now employed by the Nazis.

Back in the States, Ford is approached by U.S. intelligence agents who tell him the Nazis are rumored to have discovered the location of the Lost Ark of the Covenant (where the broken 10 Commandments were sealed). The ark is assumed to contain an awesome destructive power which Hitler ("he's a nut on the occult," we learn) is intent on using to guarantee his global conquest.

Ford's mission is to beat the Germans to the ark, a trek that takes him first to the mountains of Nepal to retrieve a hieroglyphic medallion that will pinpoint the ark's location, from his onetime flame Karen Allen. Latter, a feisty, hard-drinking spitfire, operates a Nepalese gin-mill; after a massive shootout with medallion-seeking Nazis, the pair wing it to Cairo, where Ford finally makes it to the digging ground.

The action unfolds as a continuing series of exuberantly violent and deadly confrontations – with the Nazis, hired Arab assassins, thousands of venomous snakes that guard the ark, etc., in which Ford miraculously outwits the elements in approved comic strip fashion before fending off the next round of dangers.

As such, the film has some surprisingly explicit violent action and bloodletting for a PG-rated entry and at least one scene (when the Nazis open the ark, liberating Divine fury in the form of spectral beings that melt the defilers' faces and explode their heads into smithereens) that would be attention-getting in an R-rated pic.

Still, for all but the most squeamish that won't detract an iota from the film's overall effect and the virtual start to finish grip of the off-beat tale on its viewers. Lawrence Kasdan's script (exec producer George Lucas and Philip Kaufman penned the original story) spins along the storyline, reveling in all the dialog clichés of the genre without really tipping into self-mockery. Film, cheerfully wearing its improbabilities on its sleeve, is constantly leavened by humor. The kids should love it.

Spielberg has harnessed a perfect balance between escapist fun and hard-edged action, and the film is among the best-crafted ventures of its kind. Suspense components kick in virtually from the first frame onwards, and are maintained throughout the pic.

More important, Spielberg has deftly veiled the entire proceedings in a pervading sense of mystical wonder that makes it all the more easy for viewers to willingly suspend disbelief and settle back for the fun.

Conforming to the traditions of the genre, characterizations are hardly three-dimensional. Still, Ford marks a major turning point in his career as the occasionally frail but ever invincible mercenary-archaeologist, projecting a riveting strength of character throughout. Allen's pugnacious personality provides bristling romantic counterpoint and supporting roles (including Ronald Lacey in the most outrageously offensive Nazi stereotype seen on screen since World War II, John Rhys-Davies as Ford's loyal Egyptian helpmate and Denholm Elliott as his university colleague) are all delightfully etched.

Technically, the film is another standard-setter from the Lucas-Spielberg camps (this is their first collaboration), with Douglas Slocombe's lush lensing and John Williams' dramatic score underscoring both the action and the globe-hopping epic scope.

Recruited from the "Star Wars" ranks, production designer Norman Reynolds and art director Leslie Dilley have created a vibrant and period-perfect world of wonders. Michael Kahn's crisp editing keeps the pace and energy unflagging, and Richard Edlund's photographic effects – highlighted by the apocalyptic unveiling of the ark – are intelligently spectacular.

Film's ending leaves the field wide open for a sequel (Lucas already has two more chapters up his sleeve). Hopefully the film's broad commercial promise going in will translate to a large enough bottom-line to keep his Raiders coming for a long time.

Step.

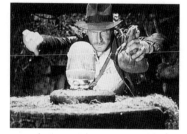

RETURN OF THE JEDI

May 18, 1983

Great creatures and effects equals smash b.o. [box office] for trilogy's finale, but weak on the human side. Hollywood, May 9. (COLOR)

A 20th Century-Fox release of a Lucasfilm Ltd. production, produced by Howard Kazanjian. Exec producer, George Lucas. Directed by Richard Marquand. Features entire cast. Screenplay, Lawrence Kasdan, George Lucas; camera (Rank Color; prints by Deluxe), Alan Hume; editors, Sean Barton, Marcia Lucas, Duwayne Dunham; sound (Dolby Stereo), Tony Dawe, Randy Thom; sound design, Ben Burtt; production design, Norman Reynolds; visual effects supervisors at Industrial Light & Magic, Richard Edlund, Dennis Muren, Ken Ralston; costumes, Aggie Guerard Rodgers, Nilo Rodis-Jamero; assistant director, David Tomblin; makeup and creature design, Phil Tippett, Stuart Freeborn; music, John Williams. Reviewed at the Academy of Motion Picture Arts & Sciences, Beverly Hills, May 9, 1983. (MPAA Rating: PG). Running time: 133 MINS.

Luke Skywalker	Mark Hamill
Han Solo	Harrison Ford
Princess Leia	Carrie Fisher
Lando Calrissian	Billy Dee Williams
C-3PO	Anthony Daniels
Chewbacca	Peter Mayhew
Emperor	Ian McDiarmid
Darth Vader	David Prowse
Vader voice	James Earl Jones
Ben Kenobi	Alec Guinness
Yoda	Frank Oz
Anakin Skywalker	Sebastian Shaw
R2-D2	Kenny Baker

Other cast: Michael Pennington, Kenneth Colley, Michael Carter, Denis Lawson, Tim Rose, Dermot Crowley, Caroline Blakiston

Additional Production Credits

Production supervisor, Douglas Twiddy; location camera, Jim Glennon; assistant directors, Roy Button, Michael Steele; art direction, Fred Hole, James Schoppe: special effects supervisor, Roy Arbogast, Kit West; stunts, Glenn Randall, Peter Diamond; choreography, Gillian Gregory; conceptual artist, Ralph McQuarrie; co-producers, Robert Watts. Jim Bloom.

Miniature & Optical Effects Unit Credits

Visual effects art direction, Joe Johnston; optical photography supervisor, Bruce Nicholson; matte-painting supervisor, Michael Pangrazio; modelshop supervisors, Lorne Peterson, Steve Gawley; visual effects editor, Arthur Repola; animation supervisor, James Keefer; stop motion animation, Tom St. Amand.

There is good news, bad news and no news about "Return Of The Jedi." The good news is that George Lucas & Co. have perfected the technical magic to a point where almost anything and everything – no matter how bizarre – is believable. The bad news is the human dramatic dimensions have been sorely sacrificed. The no news is the picture will take in millions regardless of the pluses and minuses.

As heralded, "Jedi" is the conclusion of the middle trilogy of Lucas' planned nine-parter and suffers a lot in comparison to the initial "Star Wars," when all was fresh. One of the apparent problems is neither the writers nor the principal performers are putting in the same effort.

Telegraphed in the preceding "Empire Strikes Back," the basic dramatic hook this time is Mark Hamill's quest to discover – and do something about – the true identity of menacing Darth Vader, while resisting the evil intents of the Emperor (Ian McDiarmid). Unfortunately, this sets up a number of dramatic confrontations that fall flat.

Though perfectly fine until now as daringly decent Luke Skywalker, Hamill is not enough of a dramatic actor to carry the plot load here, especially when his partner in so many scenes is really little more than an oversized gas pump, even if splendidly voiced by James Earl Jones.

Even worse, Harrison Ford, who was such an essential element of the first two outings, is present more in body than in spirit this time, given little to do but react to special effects. And it can't be said that either Carrie Fisher or Billy Dee Williams rise to previous efforts.

But Lucas and director Richard Marquand have overwhelmed these performer flaws with a truly amazing array of creatures, old and new, plus the familiar space hardware. The first half-hour, in fact, has enough menacing monsters to populate a dozen other horror pics on their own.

The good guys this time are allied with a new group, the Ewoks, a tribe of fuzzy, sweet little creatures that continually cause ahhs among the audience (and will doubtlessly sell thousands of dolls). Carrying their spears and practising primitive rites, they also allow Lucas to carry on the "Star Wars" tradition of borrowing heavily from familiar serial scenes.

Though slow to pick up the pace and

saddled with an anticlimactic sequence at the finish, "Jedi" is nonetheless reasonably fast paced for its 133-minute length, a visual treat throughout. But let's hope for some new and more involving characters in the next chapters or more effort and work for the old.

Har.

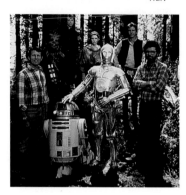

INDIANA JONES AND THE TEMPLE OF DOOM

May 16, 1984

Noisy, overkill prequel headed for smash b.o. Hollywood, May 7. (COLOR)

A Paramount Pictures release of a Lucasfilm Ltd. production. Executive producers, George Lucas, Frank Marshall. Produced by Robert Watts. Directed by Steven Spielberg. Stars Harrison Ford. Screenplay, Willard Huyck, Gloria Katz, from a story by Lucas. Camera (Rank color; prints by Deluxe), Douglas Slocombe; editor, Michael Kahn; music, John Williams; sound design (Dolby), Ben Burtt; production design, Elliot Scott; chief art director, Alan Cassie; set decoration, Peter Howitt; special visual effects supervisor, Dennis Muren at Industrial Light & Magic; costume design, Anthony Powell; mechanical effects supervisor, George Gibbs; second unit director, Michael Moore; choreography, Danny Daniels; associate producer Kathleen Kennedy. Reviewed at MGM Studios, Culver City, Calif., May 7, 1984. (MPAA Rating: PG). Running time: 118 MINS.

Indiana Jones	Harrison Ford
Willie Scott	Kate Capshaw
Short Round	Ke Huy Quan
Mola Ram	Amrish Puri
Chattar Lal	Roshan Seth
Capt. Blumburtt	Philip Stone

Also with: Roy Chiao, David Yip, Ric Young, Chua Kah Joo, Rex Ngui, Philip Tann, Dan Aykroyd, Pat Roach.

Special Visual Effects Unit Credits

Industrial Light & Magic; visual effects supervisor, Dennis Muren; chief cameraman, Mike McAlister; optical photography supervisor, Bruce Nicholson; ILM general manager, Tom Smith; production supervisor, Warren Franklin; matte painting supervisor, Michael Pangrazio; modelship supervisor, Lorne Peterson; stop-motion animation, Tom St. Amand; supervising stage technician, Patrick Fitzsimmons; animation supervisor, Charles Mullen; supervising editor, Howard Stein; production coordinator, Arthur Repola; creative consultant, Phil Tippett. Additional optical effects, Modern Film Effects.

Additional Technical Credits

U.K.crew: assistant director, David Tomblin; production supervisor, John Davis; production manager, Patricia Carr. U.S. crew: production manager, Robert Latham Brown; assistant director, Louis Race. First unit: stunt arrangers, Vic Armstrong (studio), Glenn Randall (location); additional photography, Paul Beeson; sound mixer, Simon Kaye, chief modeller, Derek Howarth; chief special effects technician, Richard Conway; floor effects supervisor, David Watkins; research, Deborah Fine; post-production services, Sprocket Systems.

London second unit: second unit director, Frank Marshall; assistant directors, David Bracknell, Michael Hook; cameraman, Wally Byatt; floor effects supervisor, David Harris.

California Unit: Second unit director, Glenn Randall; director of photography, Allen Daviau; art direction, Joe Johnston; stunt coordinator, Dean Raphael Ferrandini; special effects supervisor, Kevin Pike; sound mixer, David McMillan; production coordinator, Lata Ryan.

Asian unit: assistant director, Carlos Gil. Macau: production supervisor, Vincent Winter; production manager, Pay Ling Wang; assistant director, Patty Chan. Sri Lanka: production supervisor, Chandran Rutnam; production manager, Willie de Silva; assistant director, Ranjit H. Peiris; steadicam photography, Garrett Brown; art direction, Errol Kelly; sound mixer, Colin Charles.

Aerial unit: second unit director, Kevin Donnelly; director of photography, Jack Cooperman.

Just as "Return Of The Jedi" seemed disappointing after the first two "Star Wars" entries, so does "Indiana Jones And The Temple Of Doom" come as a letdown after "Raiders Of The Lost Ark." This is ironic, because director Steven Spielberg has packed even more thrills and chills into this followup than he did into the earlier pic, but to exhausting and numbing effect.

End result is like the proverbial Chinese meal, where heaps of food can still leave one hungry shortly thereafter. Will any of this make any difference at the boxoffice? Not a chance, as a sequel to "Raiders," which racked up $112,000,000 in domestic film rentals, has more built-in want-see than any imaginable film aside from "E.T. II."

Spielberg, scenarists Willard Huyck and Gloria Katz, and George Lucas, who penned the story as well as exec producing with Frank Marshall, have not tampered with the formula which made "Raiders" so popular. To the contrary, they have noticeably stepped up the pace, amount of incidents, noise level, budget, close calls, violence and everything else, to the point where more is decidedly less.

Prequel finds dapper Harrison Ford as Indiana Jones in a Shanghai night-club in 1935, and title sequence, which features Kate Capshaw chirping Cole Porter's "Anything Goes," looks like something out of Spielberg's "1941".

Ford escapes from an enormous mêlée with the chanteuse in tow and, joined by Oriental moppet Ke Huy Quan, they head by plane to the mountains of Asia, where they are forced to jump out in an inflatable raft, skid down huge slopes, vault over a cliff and navigate some rapids before coming to rest in an impoverished Indian village.

Community's leader implores the ace archaeologist to retrieve a sacred, magical stone which has been stolen by malevolent neighbors, so the trio makes its way by elephant to the domain of a prepubescent Maharajah, who lords it over an empire reeking of evil.

Remainder of the yarn is set in this labyrinth of horrors, where untold dangers await the heroes. Much of the action unfolds in a stupendous cavern, where dozens of natives chant wildly as a sacrificial victim has his heart removed before being lowered into a pit of fire.

Ford is temporarily converted to the nefarious cause, Ke Huy Quan is sent to join child slaves in an underground quarry, and Capshaw is lowered time and again into the pit until the day is saved.

What with John Williams' incessant score and the library full of sound effects, there isn't a quiet moment in the entire picture, and the filmmakers have piled one giant setpiece on top of another to the point where one never knows where it will end.

Film's one genuinely amazing action sequence, not unlike the airborne sleigh chase in "Jedi" (the best scene in that film), has the three leads in a chase on board an underground railway car on tracks resembling those of a roller-coaster.

Sequence represents a stunning display of design, lensing and editing, and will have viewers gaping. A "Raidersland" amusement park could be opened profitably on the basis of this ride alone.

Overall, however, pic comes on like a sledgehammer, and there's even a taste of vulgarity and senseless excess not apparent in "Raiders."

Kids 10-12 upwards will eat it all up, of course, but many of the images, particularly those involving a gruesome feast of live snakes, fried beetles, eyeball soup and monkey brains, and those in the sacrificial ceremony, might prove extraordinarily frightening to younger children who, indeed, are being catered to in this film by the presence of the adorable 12-year-old Ke Huy Quan.

Compared to the open-air breeziness of "Raiders", "Indiana Jones," after the first reel or so, possesses a heavily studio-bound look, with garish reds often illuminating the dark backgrounds.

As could be expected, however, huge production crew at Thorn EMI-Elstree Studios, as well as those on locations in Sri Lanka, Macao and California and in visual effects phase at Industrial Light & Magic, have done a tremendous job in rendering this land of high adventure and fantasy.

Ford seems effortlessly to have picked

up where he left off when Indiana Jones was last heard from (though tale is set in an earlier period), although Capshaw, who looks fetching in native attire, has unfortunately been asked to react hysterically to everything that happens to her, resulting in a manic, frenzied performance which never locates a center of gravity. Villains are all larger-than-life nasties.

Critical opinion is undoubtedly irrelevant for such a surefire commercial attraction as "Indiana Jones," except that Spielberg is such a talented director it's a shame to see him lose all sense of subtlety and nuance.

In one quick step, the "Raiders" films have gone the way the James Bond opuses went at certain points, away from nifty stories in favor of one big effect after another. But that won't prevent Spielberg and Lucas from notching another mark high on the list of alltime b.o. winners.

Cart.

INDIANA JONES AND THE LAST CRUSADE

May 24–30, 1989

Hollywood. A Paramount Pictures release of a Lucasfilm Ltd. production. Executive producers, George Lucas, Frank Marshall. Produced by Robert Watts. Production executive (U.S.), Kathleen Kennedy. Directed by Steven Spielberg. Screenplay, Jeffrey Boam, from a story by Lucas, Menno Meyjes, based on characters created by Lucas and Philip Kaufman; camera (Rank color), Douglas Slocombe; additional photography, Paul Beeson, Robert Stevens; editor, Michael Kahn; music, John Williams; sound (Dolby), Ben Burtt; production design, Elliot Scott; art direction, Stephen Scott, Richard Berger (U.S.), Benjamin Fernandez (Spain), Guido Salsilli (Italy); set design, Alan Kaye (U.S.); set decorators, Peter Howitt, Ed McDonald (U.S.), Julian Mateos (Spain); visual effects supervisor, Michael J. McAlister, Industrial Light & Magic; mechanical effects supervisor, George Gibbs; costume design, Anthony Powell, Joanna Johnston; makeup supervisor, Peter Robb-King; stunt coordinator, Vic Armstrong; associate producer, Arthur Repola; assistant directors, David Tomblin (U.K.), Dennis Maguire (U.S.), Carlos Gil, Jose Luis Escolar (Spain), Gianni Cozzo (Italy); second-unit directors, Michael Moore, Frank Marshall; second-unit camera, Rex Metz (U.S.); second-unit assistant director, Gareth Tandy (U.K.); production supervisor, Patricia Carr (U.K.); unit production managers, Roy Button (U.K.), Joan Bradshaw, Ian Bryce (U.S.), Denise O'Dell (Spain); location managers, Bruce Rush

(U.S.), Christopher Hamilton (Italy); casting, Maggie Cartier, Mike Fenton, Judy Taylor, Valerie Massalas. Reviewed at Mann National theater, L.A., May 16, 1989. (MPAA Rating: PG-13.) Running time: 127 MINS.

Indiana Jones	Harrison Ford
Professor Henry Jones	Sean Connery
Marcus Brody	Denholm Elliott
Elsa	Alison Doody
Sallah	John Rhys-Davies
Walter Donovan	Julian Glover
Young Indy	River Phoenix
Vogel	Michael Byrne
Kazim	Kevork Malikyan
Grail Knight	Robert Eddison
Fedora	Richard Young
Sultan	Alexei Sayle
Young Henry	Alex Hyde-White
Panama Hat	Paul Maxwell

To say that Paramount's "Indiana Jones And The Last Crusade" may be the best film ever made for 12-year-olds is not a backhanded compliment. What was conceived as a child's dream of a Saturday matinee serial has evolved into a moving excursion into religious myth.

More cerebral than the first two Indiana Jones films, and less schmaltzy than the second, this literate adventure should make big bucks by entertaining and enlightening kids and adults.

The Harrison Ford-Sean Connery father-and-son team gives "Last Crusade" unexpected emotional depth, reminding us that real film magic is not in special effects.

For Lucas and Spielberg, who are now entering middle age, the fact that this is more a character film than f/x extravaganza could signal a welcome new level of ambition.

Jeffrey Boam's witty and laconic screenplay, based on a story by Lucas and Menno Meyjes, takes Ford and Connery on a quest for a prize bigger than the Lost Ark of the covenant — The Holy Grail.

Connery is a medieval lit prof with strong religious convictions who has spent his life assembling clues to the Grail's whereabouts. Father and more intrepid archaeologist son piece them together in an around-the-world adventure, leading to a touching and mystical finale that echoes "Star Wars" and "Lost Horizon." The love between father and son transcends even the quest for the Grail, which is guarded by a special 700-year-old knight beautifully played by Robert Eddison.

This film minimizes the formulaic love interest, giving newcomer Alison Doody an effectively sinuous but decidedly secondary role. The principal love story is between father and son, making Ford's casually sadistic personality more sympathetic than in the previous pics.

The relationship between the men is full of tension, manifesting itself in Connery's amusing sexual one-upmanship and his string of patronizing putdowns.

There's also a warmth and growing respect between them that makes this one of the most pleasing screen pairings since Newman met Redford.

Connery confidently plays his aging character as slightly daft and fuzzy-minded, without blunting his forcefulness and without sacrificing his sexual charisma.

The cartoonlike Nazi villains of

"Raiders" have been replaced by more genuinely frightening Nazis led by Julian Glover and Michael Byrne. Most of the film takes place in 1938, and Spielberg stages a chilling scene at a Nazi book-burning rally in Berlin, where Ford has a brief encounter with Adolf Hitler.

But exec producers Lucas and Frank Marshall, producer Robert Watts and Spielberg do not neglect the action set-pieces that give these films their commercial cachet.

There's the opening chase on top of a train in the Utah desert, involving a youthful Indy (River Phoenix) in 1912; a ferocious tank battle in the desert; a ghastly scene with hundreds of rats in a Venice catacomb; some aerial hijinks with a zeppelin and small planes, and many more outlandish scenes.

Perhaps the film's most impressive technical aspect is the soundtrack, designed by Ben Burtt. While the noise level sometimes becomes painful, the artistry is stunning.

Douglas Slocombe's lensing has a subtly burnished look, and Elliott Scott's production design is always spectacular.

The Industrial Light & Magic visual effects — supervised by Michael J. McAlister with Patricia Blau producing for the aerial unit — are artful and seamless.

John Williams' score again is a major factor in the appeal and pacing, and editor Michael Kahn makes the film move like a bullet. Other tech contributions are impeccable.

This is a film of which Lucas and Spielberg and their collaborators long will be proud.

Mac.

Bibliography

The following books and articles were used, among others, as background material.

Bock, Audie, 'George Lucas, an interview', *Take One*, May 1976

Brackett, Leigh and Kasdan, Lawrence, *Star Wars: The Empire Strikes Back* (Faber & Faber, 1997)

Champlin, Charles, *George Lucas: The Creative Impulse* (Virgin, 1997)

Fairchild, Jr., B. H., *Songs of Innocence and Experience: The Blakean Vision of George Lucas*, Texas Woman's University Press

Jenkins, Garry, *Empire Building: The Remarkable Real Life Story of Star Wars* (Simon & Schuster, 1998)

Kasdan, Lawrence and Lucas, George, *Star Wars, Return of the Jedi* (Faber & Faber, 1997)

Klemesrud, Judy, 'Graffiti is the story of his life', *New York Times*, 7 October 1973

Lucas, George, *Star Wars: A New Hope* (Faber & Faber, 1997)

Pollock, Dale, 'George Lucas', *Sunday Express*, 22 May 1983

Pollock, Dale, Skywalking: *The Life and Times of George Lucas* (Samuel French, 1990)

Scanlon, Paul, 'George Lucas who plays guitar', *Rolling Stone*, 4 August 1983

Strick, Philip, 'Indiana Jones and the Temple of Doom', *Films and Filming*, July 1984

Sweeney, Louise, 'The movie business is alive and well and living in San Francisco', *SHOW*, April 1970

Thomson, David, *A Biographical Dictionary of Film* (Andre Deutsch, 3rd edn, 1994)

Tuckman, Mark and Anne Thompson, 'I'm the boss', *Film Comment*, March 1983

Vallely, Jean, 'Motion Pictures', *Rolling Stone*, 12 June 1980

Yule, Andrew, *Steven Spielberg: Father to the Man* (Little, Brown, 1996)

Zito, Stephen, 'Far Out', *American Film*, March 1977

'George Lucas' Galactic Empire', *Time*, 6 March 1978

Acknowledgements

The author would like to express his deepest thanks to all involved with this project, who gave generously of themselves at various times. Most specifically, sincerest gratitude is owed to Suzanne Fenn, Martha Jones, Dickie Jobson, Perry Henzell, Rick Elgood, Don Letts, Adrian Boot, Suzette Newman, Mark Booth, Juliet Hohnen, Trevor Dolby, Natasha Martyn-Johns, Alex and Cole (who really understand these things), the staff of London's BFI Library, Julian Alexander, Kirsten Romano and Peter Katz. May the Force be with you.

The publishers would like to thank the following for providing the pictures in this book: Capital Pictures for page 143, Katz for pages 2 and 119, Photofest for pages 6, 16, 32, 52, 59, 89 and endpapers and The Kobal Collection for pages 19, 99, 102, 114-15, 123, 125, 129, 132 and 134.

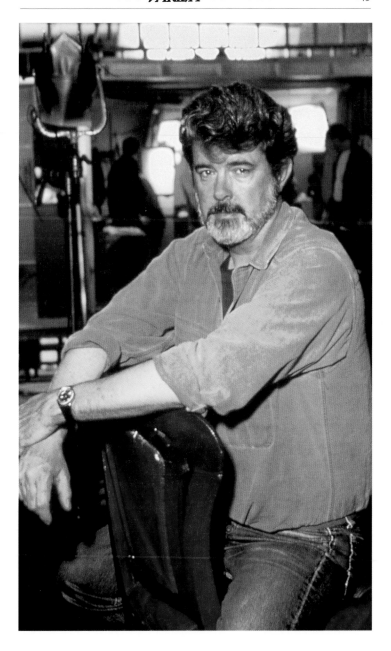